Parenting Better Children

An 8-Week Skills Training Program
Guide To Reach, Teach & Empower

Jennifer L. Wilke-Deaton, MA, LPA

I love her simple, concrete examples that make even the most complex parent/child interactions accessible and doable. I would sign up for this class as I no doubt would glean even more insight into working with my own clients.

– Brian R. King, LCSW
Author of *the Perfect Moments in Relationships:*
Lessons in Connection for Work, Family, Love, and Life

Jennifer Wilke-Deaton has developed a fantastic resource for clinicians working with children and families. Her step by step 'Parenting Course' takes the reader through a well-organized, easy to apply program. Jen's perspective, drawn from years of clinical expertise, along with the detailed research she presents makes this book truly credible and applicable to today's parenting challenges.

– Susan P. Epstein, LCSW
author of *55 Creative Approaches for Challenging & Resistant Children & Adolescents*
and *Over 60 Techniques, Activities & Worksheets for Challenging Children & Adolescents*

Weaving together her practical clinical experience and current research, Jennifer provides cleanly organized parenting strategies for both parents and clinicians. This class provides highly effective techniques I share on a daily basis with parents of youth involved in the juvenile justice system.

– L.C. Jones, Attorney
Juvenile Specialist

Jennifer Wilke-Deaton has hit a home-run with this practical blueprint for improving parental success in the most common circumstances. She has standardized the basics and still managed to leave room for flexibility, so families can truly adapt these lessons to meet the needs of the particular challenges in their own home environment. I really like the movement away from reliance on arbitrary tokens to manage behavior and the focus on intentional relationship building to set new norms for family success. This will definitely improve our work to strengthen youth and family connections in the field.

– Hasan Davis, J.D.,
former commissioner of Kentucky Department
of Juvenile Justice and Child and Family Advocate

Jennifer Wilke-Deaton, MA, LPA, is a licensed behavioral health therapist working in a private practice setting in Richmond, KY. Jen has more than 15 years of experience working with crisis management, psychological testing, inpatient/outpatient treatment, groups, families, and the court system. A tireless and passionate advocate for children and families, she developed a parent training program recognized by the Governor's Commission for the Treatment of Children &Families and Kentucky's Child Protective Services. Jen helped create a regional children's crisis stabilization unit, children's advocacy center, and an intensive after-school program for behaviorally-challenged youth. She has published *the Creative Parenting Handbook, CD Awareness In Focus: Modern Guided Imagery Techniques for Immediate Practice, CD Awareness in Focus By Kids For Kids, and The Mandala Workbook: Activities Across the Lifespan.*

In addition to delivering her nationally recognized training programs for PESI/CMI and keynote presentations, Jen regularly speaks on mental health issues and child abuse for Morehead State University, Eastern Kentucky University, KY Child Protective Services, and National Public Radio; as well as providing psychological evaluations and therapeutic services for the Department of Disability Determinations and the Office of Vocational Rehabilitation. Jennifer consults regularly for private/state foster care organizations, social services, schools, psychiatric hospitals, Head Start programs, in-home therapy programs, and case management services. Her specialties are in the areas of child abuse, PTSD, DBT, behavioral disorders, anxiety, autistic spectrum, and attachment. Jen shares time-tested, real approaches from the trenches, using humor, energy and passion for helping others.

Dedication

To my beautiful and precocious daughter, Ella,
who has given me perspective about parenting that
I never would have gained without her.
To my husband, David, who supports me in every single endeavor without fail.
To my mother-in-law, Geraldine, for her insight, patience, and knowledge.
To my sister, LeAnn, who gave of her time generously (hours of playing princess, ponies
and dress-up) so that this book could make it onto the pages.
My Grams.
And to the rest of my friends and family, who challenge me each day
to be a better person and more effective clinician.
I am eternally grateful for you all!

Published by
PESI Publishing and Media
PESI, Inc.
3839 White Ave
Eau Claire, WI 54703

Cover Design: Amy Rubenzer
Layout: Kayla Huset
Editing: Kayla Huset

Printed in the United States of America

ISBN: 978-1-937661-60-1

PESI
Publishing
& Media
www.pesipublishing.com

Author's Notes

As I have traveled around the US and taught individuals in the helping profession for the past decade; my insight to the problems facing our youth, and the needs of their care providers and families has expanded exponentially. I have been privileged to meet people in all capacities, from teachers, clinicians, and residential staff to occupational therapists, speech/language pathologists, and parents. All of whom are compelled to make the effort to help our children and youth in the best way we possibly can. I have met people hungry for more knowledge and eager to learn new techniques for helping all they come in contact with. As I often say at the start of my seminars, we are all colleagues and teachers. We are all working in the trenches, doing the very best we can to help improve the lives of those we have been given the responsibility to better. I know the people I have been honored to meet take this charge seriously. The desire to offer the most well-informed and empirically researched tools they possibly can is apparent in the many questions I answer, troubleshooting I try to offer for specific cases, and the emails I respond to. I am eternally appreciative of the contacts with all of these individuals, as they truly inspire me to attempt to think outside of the box and endeavor to find the most efficient way to communicate often difficult concepts in ways that are easily applied in diverse settings.

I, too, am constantly searching for something new and inspiring to engage the families and children I work with on a daily basis. I attend seminars as well, hoping to glean information and experience different ways of thinking about tools for kids to be the very best they can be. I am passionate in the belief that we all have the capacity to improve our ability to live in this ever changing world. This is our world of unpredictability, overwhelming expectations, and uncertain futures. It is a world that our children and our children's children will inherit, and it is our duty to prepare them in the best way we possibly can to achieve and endeavor to be amazing.

As a practicing clinician, I hear many complaints and experience a barrage of referrals for children with behavioral problems. Quite frankly, many of the issues that I hear of with children and families are similar concerns I too have had as a parent. I find myself asking these questions in my own household. "How do I get them to listen to me?" "Why do they seem to behave so well with other people, and I struggle with their behaviors at home?" "What am I doing that's wrong?" "Is it me?" I often experience feelings of frustration with our mental health and educational systems (of which I am a part) on a daily basis. Not only do we as professionals, but also many exhausted parents, have a common core problem "How do we help these kids when we feel like we have tried everything?" In my practice, I find that we so often point the finger of blame at parents and teachers in these children's lives. This kind of approach has led to a long-term sense of disempowerment and invalidation. Many of the families and professionals that I work with are fatigued and overwhelmed with the responsibility of caring for these kids. I constantly ask myself how we can help develop people's desire, increased drive, and promote sustained effort while working with children; when the internal experience and self-perception is "I am failing."

I find that I have continued concerns regarding our approaches to parent training and classroom management. Over the past 15–20 years we have developed a continued dependency on secondary gain-driven systems, which focus primarily on compliance rather than developing internal drive and a model of prevention. My greatest frustration about these types of programs is that they create a society of poorly centered and self-aware children who carry these values into adulthood. We've taken the demand for brief treatment intervention to the very farthest degree, as these techniques are often easily understood and applied, and have unintentionally fueled and developed a relatively severe and difficult to stabilize behavioral population (Deci et al., 2001; Cameron,

1994). Over time, these types of behaviors, if not adapted and intervened, could potentially develop more rigid and difficult to treat behavioral issues and personality features (Eitam, 2008; Eisenburger, et al, 1999).

Firstly, many of the behavioral programs in schools, homes, psychiatric facilities, detention sites, and counseling centers have been based on obtaining tangible and external rewards. We have prided ourselves on developing different types of token economies, point systems, leveling programs, and other behavioral purchasing plans over the past several years, which generally work for a brief period of time and in the end fail to create an environment of self-driven positive behavior (Lieberman, 2000; Ayllon, 1999; Alyord, 1998; Maslow, 1987). These types of systems often are open to manipulation or "cheating" by the target population, and result in feelings of entitlement with little understanding for the necessity of living effectively in your world (Pintrich, 2003; Weist, 2001; Murphy et al., 2000). Token economies are actually a wonderful program for daycare, preschool, and grade school settings, but were intended to be used for a short period of time to increase children's understanding of classroom rules and the daily schedule. Point systems, which are often utilized in residential settings and therapeutic detention sites, are based on the gains/losses concept of behavioral management. Unfortunately, these types of systems are more often based on losses rather than gains. Earnings-based systems are far more effective in developing positive self-esteem and intrinsic desire, but also become quite complicated and difficult for parents to manage on a daily basis, especially with increased home responsibilities for academics. It is unfortunate that these types of programs have been divvied out to families and school systems without proper theoretical comprehension and guidance of effective long-term application. I have professionally found that these programs have excellent intentions, but are generally underdeveloped and overgeneralized to large populations. These programs fail because of their lack of individualization and the ability to generalize skills to multiple settings (Hagger, 2011; Gillet, 2012).

A broader concern is that point and token systems often utilize tangible reinforcements as part of the contingency (i.e. poker chips, points, buttons, rocks, stickers, etc.) that are in no way connected to the behavior that is being trained. Research has been quite clear about the importance of immediate feedback as a necessity to adjust and develop healthy and efficient cognition. The process of immediate and relatable feedback can actually help develop hardwired neural connections in the brain (Foerde, 2013; Shute, 2007). People using these systems have the basic understanding that feedback must be given to the individual, but what they are missing is that not only does the feedback from the environment need to be immediate, but also needs to be related to the initiating behavior (Mathan, 2003; Kagan, 2001; Mesulam, 1997; Benton, 1968). For example, how do the 100 points earned over several hours or days, which are then used to purchase stickers or balloons from a "store," have anything to do with developing positive communication or self-regulation?

If you know children whose behaviors are being managed by point systems or token economies, you also know that the thought of losing representative points can frequently provoke anxiety, create dishonesty, and even increase aggressive behaviors due to agitation and low frustration tolerance. This is exactly the opposite of what we are trying to achieve through these models of intervention. Often, children experience feelings of "unfairness" or deep loss when participating in systems as those aforementioned. I also hear comments from the children that I work with, such as, "I'm saving up my points to get something really good." Never mind that being trusted and having the respect of people should generally be considered a "really good" experience. By the time children have earned the amount necessary to purchase goods or extra privileges, the importance of the positive behavior itself is often lost in the process of earning "things." This is why I believe that we have many children and adolescents saying to us, while holding their hands out, "I'll be good, but what do I get for it?" I would also venture to say that these types of approaches have created an increasingly entitled society, which has a constant expectation for reinforcement of basic living. Now the idea of "extra special earnings" has just become a daily norm, and can make the process of finding meaningful reinforcements quite difficult for parents and staff.

These systems of behavioral rewarding and consequences also rarely have much in common with real-world experiences. Experiences such as reciprocal relationships, educational achievement, and volunteerism or altruism (aka kindness) get missed in the process. One of our goals should be to develop behavioral patterns that can be practiced in many places consistently. Generalized and well-practiced behaviors are the longest lasting, and we already see this with negative behaviors with our child behavior populations. Children have already been reinforced for their own negative behaviors for so many years. The pattern of reinforcement needs to be addressed and adapted to understanding that positive behaviors can earn them so much more in the long run. Generally, we adults do not earn tangible rewards for everything that we do. As parents, clinicians, and school staff our focus needs to shift in the direction of developing intrinsic desire for "doing the right thing" not because we're getting something for it, but because it feels good. Being "positive" often times takes far more effort than being "negative," but in the end, it creates positive self-concept, acceptance and engagement from our social environment, and the ability to regulate internally. These types of reinforced experiences foster opportunities for development of far greater benefit than a Dora the Explorer® sticker or a SpongeBob SquarePants® temporary tattoo.

The research over the past 15–20 years has begun to focus on the need for developing emotional IQ skills to impact characterological development in youth populations (Hayes, 2013; Webb, 2013; Fiori, 2011 & 2002). We must begin to highlight the importance of developing skills of self-efficacy, positive self-esteem and self-worth, kindness, respect, autonomy, empathy/remorse, and work ethic. Many of the parenting/staff programs that I have witnessed are focused primarily on strict compliance, when at times it's not always healthy or safe for our children to "do exactly as we are told the first time (i.e. gang participation, sexual victimization, and substance use/abuse)." This is not to say that we throw out the horse and the cart, as it is perfectly appropriate to have some external rewards as a fringe benefit. It's always fun to have tangible rewards from our environment, but to have an expectation that this will be the constant is unrealistic and setting up our children for disappointment and failure in the future. These types of rewards lose their significance when they are taken for granted as part of daily life, and hence become far less meaningful.

My second area of concern is that due to the demands for short-term and brief treatment interventions, we as clinicians have become more advisers than counselors to our clients. It is clearly our responsibility, as well as a necessary component of effective and long-lasting behavioral treatment, to challenge individuals to create their own solutions for their needs to be met with direction. By removing this component of cognitive challenge, we also lose the opportunity to nurture positive and independent thought and effective internal problem-solving skills. This is especially important when thinking about neurobiological research, and the understanding that prefrontal cortex function is responsible for higher order learning/processing and executive functioning skills

(Stuss, 2013; Goldman-Racik, 2006; Wagner, 2001; Robert, 1988). By removing the component of linking together verbal direction with hands on, or practice-based, application of new skills and techniques, we also take away the opportunity to develop higher prefrontal cortex function. This is especially impaired in our child and family populations that have auditory and verbal processing disorders. It is unrealistic to have an expectation that someone with these types of processing issues might be able to immediately understand, apply, and practice new skills based on verbal directive alone (Pierce, 2013; Mashal, 2012; Mate, 2012; Wooley, 2010). It is our responsibility to allow for application of techniques and practice of tools in real world settings, to increase the likelihood of neurological change in response to skills training.

Many of the families and children that I've worked with have been in and out of the revolving door of clinical treatment for years. We have developed a dependency on others for answering our problems for us, instead of giving us autonomous abilities to problem-solve and live effectively in our worlds without the necessity of treatment. Many of the families I have had an opportunity to come in contact with have a history of successful achievement of their therapeutic goals during the duration of treatment, but return to therapy within months or weeks because they do not feel confident in independently applying their skills or utilizing resources. This is likely due to the approach of giving a laundry list of reinforcers and consequences to families and schools, rather than individualizing plans and promoting a healthy understanding that mistakes are an opportunity for change. Recognition is the first step to movement in a positive direction, and recovery in family systems can often be a long-term process; especially when you begin recognizing the impact of normal developmental changes and environmental stresses. Remember that we all can make mistakes, and mistakes are our way of reflecting on areas that require more focus or needs for change.

In my intensive afterschool program we made a clear distinction between "coping skills," which are effective de-escalation and self-regulation tools that are easily accessed; and then we have something called "coping skills-schmoping skills," which are the things that we have been told *should* be useful but are not necessarily effective based on their individual needs or matching of their abilities. For example, one child might "take deep breaths" or "count to 10" and that may be effective and useful for them without a great deal of assistance, but for others these types of skills may be perceived as impossible to utilize. Therefore, the goal is to find what works for each person individually and develop those skills specifically, so that they do not require the constant reminder of "now you are supposed to take deep breaths or count to 10." Part of this responsibility, again, is practicing these skills instead of simply talking about them. Without the practice component, we have essentially failed our children and families who have issues with auditory processing skills and the need for hands-on application of new tools.

Also, many of the techniques that we incorporate into behavioral plans are not specific to the environmental factors that are occurring at the time (i.e. classroom disruption, economic impact in the home, physical illness, etc.) For example, Joey has a problem with the use of foul language. Timeout (now referenced in this text as "cool-down time") may be effective and appropriate if he initiated the solution himself, but if the rest of the students in the classroom initiated the use of foul language then timeout only serves to isolate Joey rather than develop positive communication in the classroom setting. Timeout as it is being practiced currently by many parents and staff is an effective method of removing a child from harming themselves or other people, but it does not meet the needs of managing all behavioral problems in all settings. In fact, the effort of adults should be focused on the prevention of triggering the incident in the first place to avoid the need for this type of punishment, which is often a short-lived solution to the problem. We need to focus on parent and staff training that teaches the basic concepts and building blocks of individualized positive parenting (and yes, teachers "parent" too). We must teach ourselves to train those concepts and give parents and staff the opportunity to practice and gain feedback, so that they are able to apply these skills to a multitude of behaviors and settings independently.

My goal for this parenting book is to assist professionals, and that includes clinicians and teachers,

in their ability to teach, allow the practice of skills, and then troubleshoot difficulties for anyone working with behavioral concerns. Not all behavioral problems have to be clinically significant, and honestly the goal should be to manage the behavior before it becomes clinically significant. It is important to set a goal for yourself as a professional of focusing on empowerment for the disempowered, validating the invalidated, reassuring the fearful, and supporting those that need assistance in the journey of learning new skills. Anyone working with children also needs to be responsive to immediate feedback from participants, and to feel a sense of self-worth and efficacy when teaching and making their own mistakes in the leadership role. In doing this, you will experience greater openness not only to initial and ongoing treatment, but also to one's comfort in asking for assistance rather than advice if, and when, things become difficult. I frequently refer to this behavior of requesting assistance with parents as "getting boosters" and with staff as "someone having your back." Rather than feeling the desire to give up and start from scratch again, we want to nurture an environment of acceptance amongst ourselves and the notion that "things just change sometimes."

The following book includes the basic structure of effective foundational parenting training, not just for parents but for educational professionals and staff in residential facilities. As the weeks of treatment progress you will find that as a team you develop more positive parenting skills on a stable basis of building blocks, rather than starting to train parenting late in the process of well-practiced negative behaviors and frustrated staff interventions, which constitutes an unstable foundation. We will focus our attention on going back to the basics to avoid the constant and frequent repairs that come with dependency on "the system." I wish you the best of luck with these individuals and I know that you will experience great success.

Introduction

After growing up in the suburbs of Chicago and moving my career path to rural Appalachia Kentucky, I realized that the needs of parents were basically the same everywhere I went. In taking the time to get to know the families and the communities that I lived in, I discovered that our parent population was one of the most underserved groups of individuals in every place. It didn't matter if they lived in a rural community or in urban centers, we had people that felt that they were failing kids everywhere. Here we were sending children to treatment facilities, psychiatric hospitals, and making referrals for intensive therapy only to have them return to homes and school-systems that were falling apart within a few short months. I often find myself asking, "What do we need to do for this family/community/school system to help them be successful after these kids return from finishing all this hard work in intensive treatment?" It seemed inconceivable that we might be harming the children we treated by setting them up for failure at their discharge time, but it was happening. I continue to have parents that come to my office, hair askew, bags under their eyes, and with deflated posture that say, "Jen, just tell me what to do. . .I don't understand why nothing seems to work to help my child. What is the answer?"

When I reflected on these types of questions, I realized that they were absolutely right. We, as clinicians and other professionals, have constantly been treating behavioral problems as if they were a disease. We approach treatment as a medical professional rather than focusing on the system of dysfunction, and recognizing that we all have individual strengths and weaknesses. By reflecting on these thoughts and gaining an awareness of our professional weaknesses, I decided to stop doing what was *not ever going to work*, and start focusing on tools and techniques that create a new way of thinking and being in our world, rather than just responding to behaviors. Through research, observation, and sampling, I created

this foundational parenting program. I continue to be passionate about making efforts towards offering support, educating, and guiding parents in a validating way through the process of positive parenting and empowerment. I still make mistakes, as we all do. I still believe that the very best way to learn is to make those kinds of mistakes, recognize them, and then adapt.

Many of the parents that we work with are more comfortable with failing than achieving. I could never find a program for parent training that addressed both skills training as well as the frustration and confusion associated with experiencing change (whether it be "good" or "bad"). This program was created to structure the way parents and staff communicate with children, identify their own needs that must be met for a realistic expectation for success, have a place to appropriately vent and receive support and validation, and find answers to questions they didn't even realize they had at times (Koemer, 2013; Perepletchikova, 2011; Linehan, 2002 & 1994). This parenting program is structured in an 8-week, one hour a week, group session. I have in the past, for the sake of schedules and billing restrictions, cut the program down to a four-week, two hour a week group. In doing this though, I only experienced more perceived failure and frustration within my parents. I can see now that this is likely due to the learning curve and standards for group rapport building. I found that in week four of this eight-week course lights seemed to just "turn on" for parents and staff. At that time, group members have stopped being invested in the anger over previous failures (as well as having to attend yet *another* parenting class) and have a tendency to become more motivated, engaged, and driven to achieve. Approximately 90% of the families and facilities that have participated in this parent training program reported experiencing positive growth, a sense of autonomy, and long-term parental/staff success, without the necessity for directed treatment or outside consultation. I continue to hear from these parents, teachers, and staff who at times require boosters and answers to questions as their kids grow and change, but their awareness of these changes and the expectation that flexibility is a necessity as a care provider serves them well.

Remember that this is an empirically-based parent skills training group. By being flexible, which can require that clinicians and teachers understand the demands of alternative techniques for the basic building blocks, and responding to the needs of each group as a separate entity, you will experience much greater and long-lasting success. That is what our parents are asking for, and that is what we are capable of giving them.

What follows is:

1. An outline for clinicians and teachers with a clearly structured program for each week of face-to-face time.

2. Discussion points and troubleshooting. One of the most important components of each week is your troubleshooting and information gathering section, so that you can address and flexibly respond to the needs of that specific group.

3. An outline for parents and handouts (intended to be copied for use), so that they have a nice visual cue helping them to remember "oh yeah, this is what we are talking about this week" or "this is what I'm supposed to be trying out at home before I come back the next time."

4. Examples to illustrate each key point. I have attempted to offer you examples to utilize for each week, but also challenge you to consider using direct examples from the group table.

5. A graduation certificate. Surprisingly, one of the most important pages that you have in this book is a certificate of completion. When you hand this to a parent at the end of your eight weeks of face time, you will see a sort of giddy relief. It also serves as a reminder (visual cue) that they learned something different to try even in the heat of the moment at home.

Before you begin your first week, it is especially important that you have screened parents or staff members individually, so that you know that they are intellectually and emotionally capable of participating in the group training. Also be sure to obtain any releases that are to be signed for the court system or social services. Let them know that their behavior and participation may be shared with these people specifically, but only because they gave you permission to do so.

Outline

Week 1

Our First Meeting

The Basics of Behavioral Change
Need for a Predictable Routine
Effective Use of Cool-Down Time

Week 1

Parenting Skills Outline

Our First Meeting

- Introductions and address parents' frustrations without allowing "gripe session" to occur.

- Discuss confidentiality and group participation expectations. Be sure to clarify that group is a place of safety and privacy. I often say, "A place for you to feel supported without concern that the information will leave the room, or that you will be judged."

  1. **Handout:** Confidentiality Agreement For Parenting Class

- Validation of parents' discipline history, argument styles, how they were disciplined as children, as well as the ages of the children with which you are working.

- Introduce Consistency, Reinforcement, Punishment, and Bribery: (standard for all ages)

  1. Definition of **Consistency**: "Always doing the same thing, the same way, every time."

     a. Use applicable examples

     b. Give the timeline for expected change over 30 days.

  2. Definition of **Reinforcement**: "A tool to increase a behavior's likelihood of happening."

     a. Note that you can increase negative and positive behaviors alike (grocery store example).

  3. Definition of **Punishment**: "A tool that decreases a behavior's likelihood of happening." (Example of non-physical punishment, too.)

     a. Note that physical punishment is short lasting and the least effective parenting technique to utilize.

        i. Average effect is three days of decreased behavior before negative behaviors return.

     b. Physical punishment increases the likelihood of aggressive behavioral responses to other children in academic and daycare settings.

  4. Definition of **Bribery**: "Providing reinforcement *before* the expected behaviors occur." (Example of court bribery.)

     a. Bribery increases the chances that an expected behavior will *not* occur.

     b. Bribery is a method of manipulation for children (example: "If you give me a cookie first, then I will clean my room." The room never gets cleaned, because the item was given before the expected behavior).

- Re-introduce timeout, now referenced as "**Cool-Down Time**" (most effective for ages 3–12). Timeout was initially intended to be an opportunity to cool down before escalation, but now has been used as a punishment for several years. Internally, children connect the language of "timeout" with a negative experience, so changing the language and how we label this experience decreases the potential for a negative internal reference.

1. The five rules of "**Cool-Down Time**" (Handout). Recognize that for many parents, they do not believe that timeout techniques work because it has failed in the past. Note that they haven't followed all of the steps, and that is likely why it has not worked *yet*.

    i. *Cool-down should occur in a place free from outside stimulation and interruption.*

        a. Effective places:

            i. A specific chair in the kitchen identified by a string (not the same chair that they eat in, and no distracting items on the table such as mail or groceries).

            ii. A doorway in the hallway away from other children, pets, television, computers, or video games.

        b. Ineffective places:

            i. Their bedroom (where they have toys and you expect them to sleep without an internal connection to punishment).

            ii. The middle of the living room.

    ii. *Never respond to a child in cool-down, unless it is a safety issue.*

        a. Remember that reinforcement can come in the form of meeting the need for attention-seeking (even eye contact and proximity to their behavior is a reinforcement).

        b. You can verbalize minimally, but only as necessary, "You are taking a cool-down, and your time does not start until you are quiet."

        c. If they speak or move from the cool-down location state, "*Your cool-down starts over from the beginning.*"

    iii. *One minute for every year of age.*

        a. Never more than one minute per year, or children get overwhelmed and distracted by the time itself. Feel free to adapt the time for younger children, with limited attention.

        b. With very young children, under the age of 6, we often allow for children to discontinue sitting in cool-down time when they have become less upset (have self-regulated). This is a positive reinforcement for the behavior of learning to calm independently.

    iv. *The adult is not responsible for keeping time in cool-down time.*

        a. Effective timers: Because the child does not have to ask continually, "Is my time up yet?" = Reinforcement of the negative behavior. To decrease the likelihood of reinforcing the questioning behavior, you must set the timer and walk away.

            i. Microwave timer.

            ii. Stove timer.

            iii. Cell phone timer.

            iv. Windup egg timer.

            v. Anything that makes a sound at the end of cool-down.

        b. Ineffective timers: Because you can't hear if the child tampers with the time, and it also opens a doorway for inconsistency.

            i. Parent/child watches (parents get distracted and forget the time)

            ii. Wall clock, especially if children are unable to tell time by analog clock.

            iii. No timer at all = guessing game.

v. *The* <u>most important part</u> *is processing or* ***"talking it out"*** *after cool-down is over.*

    a. *Immediately* following cool-down, address the child and ask, "Why were you in cool-down?"

    b. Allow the child to recall, without answering for them. Three tries to recall, then assist.

    c. Then ask, "What could you do the next time, so you don't have to have a cool-down time?"

    d. Process every cool-down. They know what they *can't* do, now teach them what they *can* do. When we tell children things we *don't* want them to do, we leave them hanging with questions of "Well, what am I supposed to do?" (e.g. "Walk down the hallway," rather than "Stop running.")

- The importance of a **predictable routine** to increase attachment and bonding between parental figures and children.

    1. Sleep Routines

        i. Having a regular bedtime schedule and routine assists with regulating circadian rhythm, which in turn can decrease behavioral problems, irritability, and agitation.

        ii. Having a regular bedtime ritual offers opportunities for parents and children to decompress after the day is done, and prepare for the following day.

    2. Meal Planning and Eating

        i. Having a meal at the table with family members, rather than in front of the television set, allows families to become more aware of eating behaviors, which can decrease issues related to childhood obesity.

        ii. Having a meal at the table with family members also offers an opportunity for open conversation about peer selection, school issues, and family planning for the daily routine.

    3. Exercising Together

        i. Having regular physical activity together assists families in decreasing the negative impact of high levels of technology on brain function.

        ii. This activity doesn't have to be an organized sport. Simply taking a walk together, or having sit-up or squatting competitions can be enough physical activity to change the brain response to parent-child interactions.

        iii. Having regular physical activity as a family also offers an opportunity for team building as a family system and developing awareness of strengths within the family system.

    4. Engagement

        i. By having time set aside each day when family members interact one-on-one, the family system strengthens through an understanding that "my mom/dad are interested and available to me."

        ii. By engaging your children through activities like game night or family chore completion, you allow children to explore positive activities with adult leadership = decreases likelihood of negative peer seeking for validation. (Even if it's only five minutes a day, it is time *just for them*.)

        iii. Be careful to avoid over-engagement (i.e. two-hour family meetings, five-hour car rides with required conversation the entire time), so as to allow for appropriate family downtime.

Week 1

Troubleshooting/Validation

Many parents attending parenting classes for the first time are overwhelmed and anxious about expectations for group attendance and participation. Several of the parents that I have worked with have attended many different parenting classes in the past, only to leave feeling overwhelmed and de-valued. The importance of validating parents, their own personal parenting experiences, and the way that they communicate these difficulties cannot be emphasized enough. Cognitive Behavioral and Dialectical Behavioral Therapy interventions focus intensely on the notion of "validation" as an opportunity to increase the likelihood of engagement in treatment, as well as maintenance of long-term success. Many of the parents and staff we work with have lived in an invalidating environment for so many years (i.e. "You are a terrible parent for talking to them that way," "You must be an awful teacher to think that about this child"), that simply telling them that "it's okay to feel this way and/or be overwhelmed" is a salve to the injuries sustained while attempting to be an effective parent/teacher.

I also have a conversation regarding the importance of attachment in connection with your children. I validate parents and the idea that they would not even walk into a parenting class, did they not have a motivation (even if court-ordered) to remain as a caretaker for their children. We discuss openly how busy schedules in the home and behaviors of eating in front of the television or disconnecting through cell phones and video games can damage our relationships with our children. As a group we discuss the importance of connected mealtimes, sleep schedules, engagement, and exercise as an opportunity to build a family as a functional system. When working with higher functioning parent populations and staff training, I often discuss Dyadic Developmental interventions for treatment of attachment. Specifically, this model of intervention focuses on the need to have a regular and predictable routine in your world to increase the likelihood of identifying and meeting needs *before* rage or aggression is required by a child to communicate those said needs. The only way to identify needs in children is to create time to identify, reflect upon, and label these needs.

I find that by sitting in the round and placing myself as a peer rather than a leader helps initiate positive rapport more quickly. Many of the parents and staff that I have worked with tell me that they are embarrassed when they first come to group, and feel like they are the only ones having the problems that they do. I try to provide coffee or small snacks to make the atmosphere more conducive to conversation. The goal is to remove the pointing figure and the invalidating experience from the face of our parents and staff and essentially say to them, "I am here for you, we are here for each other, and you are not alone."

It is important to immediately identify the guidelines for prompt attendance, confidentiality, and your expectation for individuals in interacting with others in public places. I support the parents in their endeavor to feel accepted by others in the group, but make it clear that if they discuss names, information, or other people's children outside of group then they will be asked to discontinue participation. I emphasize the need for everyone's sense of safety and acceptance in the group setting, which also means there will be appropriate language and respectful treatment of all members of the group. Lack of respect towards others is grounds for removal. This does at times seem a bit uncalled for, but many parents and staff can and will act as inappropriately with others as their children do at times.

One of my favorite group rapport building tasks that you will do on this day is to discuss how everyone else was parented or disciplined as a child. This conversation can lead to an opportunity for validating their own experiences, avoidance of "being like my mom or dad," and create comfort and a sense of connection with other group members. Do not be surprised when they say, "My parents beat my tail off. . .I don't know why I can't just do it the same way." You may also hear, "My parents were very strict with me, so I never wanted to be like them." This is why the sections on timelines and the differences between reinforcement, punishment, and bribery are extremely important.

Parents who are referred by the court or social services systems are often quite angry and resentful when discussing their experience with "the system" (of which they often believe you are a part). I allow these parents to vent briefly while teaching them to "make the best of a bad situation." As a firm moderator, I have had to refocus several individuals to the goal of helping their child, rather than using that energy for resistance. These individuals are less apt to participate initially, and I make it clear that success comes from group conversation and participation. They are expected to participate, even if the only statement they make is "I don't see how that would work at all!" or even, "This is a bunch of BS." This is your opportunity to step in and review what has or has not worked for them, and gives the moderator a chance to engage them in a conversation about troubleshooting difficulties.

During this first week, parents regularly discuss their issues with "timeout." They often say, "I have tried everything and timeout really doesn't work." Identify the steps of timeout that they have been using in the past, as well as the likelihood that they have missed the important steps of processing. I tell parents, "Children have so many things that they know *not* to do that it is important to teach them the things that they *can* do." I also take this opportunity to discuss the impact of body positioning and eye contact on interactions with your children. For example, having your hands on your hips or arms crossed over your chest can be perceived as threatening and authoritarian by your children. This is your chance to role-play eye-level communication, open body posture, and positive "rather than drilling" eye contact. Even tired or angry eyes, or heavy sighing, can communicate negative feelings to children and others that perhaps were not intended by the adults.

The first week of group will be a tight week for time. You may need a few extra minutes to confirm that everyone knows what they need to practice before they return the following week. Practice does not in fact make perfect, but it does offer you an opportunity to make changes and assist families and school-systems to be more successful in their efforts.

HOMEWORK WEEK 1: Practice the "New and Improved" Cool-Down Time, and adjust the routine in the house (even if it's just one area at a time) while keeping track with the handout.

(With older children: Practice processing information and coming up with challenging options for adolescents.)

Confidentiality Agreement
for Parenting Class

I, _____, agree to keep all information from this parenting class private and confidential. I understand that discussion of names of attendees and their children, as well as specific examples of parenting problems mentioned by group participants within the group setting, is breaking this agreement of privacy. Should I discuss this information outside of class, without prior approval from the other attendee, my participation in group will be terminated. I understand that it is important for all group members to feel a sense of security and safety in openly discussing their parenting issues in the group setting. I understand that we all will be signing this document, and any infringement of these rules will immediately be disclosed to the group leader.

If I have been referred to this parenting class from the court system or social services, I understand that my attendance and participation records may or may not be shared with workers from these locations. Should a request be made for information regarding my group participation, I will be notified by the group leader prior to this disclosure.

_____   _____
Group Participant Signature   Date

_____   _____
Group Leader Signature   Date

Week #1

Handout for Parents

The 5 Rules of Cool-Down Time

1. Cool-down happens in a place with no noise, distractions, or interruptions.

2. Never respond to a child in cool-down (unless it is a safety issue).

3. One minute for every year your child is old, unless they calm more quickly, then feel free to pull them out for "talking it out" earlier.

4. You are not responsible for keeping time in cool-down.

5. Be sure to "talk it out."
   a. *"Why were you in cool-down?"*

   b. *"What could you do the next time, so you don't have to cool-down?"*

Week #1

Handout for Parents

Changing Your Routine

	Last Week:	This Week:
1. Bedtime was at	_____	_____
2. We had dinner at the table together as a family	#_____	#_____
3. We exercised together	#_____	#_____

4. We did these activities together as a family this week:

_____

_____

_____

Week 1

Examples and Discussion Points

Example 1: Consistency

Consistency can be considered "being a person of your word." If you don't follow through on discipline or a direction (empty threats) then you are likely *not* to be taken seriously by your child. This leads to disbelief that you really mean what you are saying.

1. You say, "If you do that one more time, you won't be allowed to stay up late." The child continues to misbehave, and you never send them to bed. That is being inconsistent.

2. If you say to your child, "If you hit your brother one more time, you won't be allowed to go to the football game tonight," and then follow through, you have made that experience meaningful for your child.

Example 2: Reinforcement

You can increase negative behaviors as well as positive behaviors, because reinforcement always increases the likelihood of a behavior happening.

1. You tell your child, "If you are good in the grocery store, then I will get you some M&Ms." They enter the store and start to misbehave in the produce isle. You say, "Remember, you have to be good to get your treat." (At that point they should have already lost the reward). They continue to misbehave throughout the store, but suddenly they see the candy at the checkout. They behave well for approximately ten feet, and you give them their candy. You have essentially rewarded misbehavior throughout the grocery store, because that was the requested behavior from the start. Chances are, the next time they go into the grocery store with you, they will misbehave while thinking "I know how to get the candy from you at the end."

2. It is important to avoid giving a child something every time they do what is expected, as the child will be less likely to behave the first time you are unable to provide a reward for their behavior (or are distracted by another activity). This is an example of continuous reinforcement contingencies, which often fail following the first missed reinforcement. This type of reinforcement creates a belief that "they deserve" something special for every move they make. Intermittent or ratio reinforcement contingencies are often most effective, because the behavior will continue in a positive way without a direct expectation of immediate reinforcement (i.e. the use of several different kinds of reinforcements or the slot machine effect).

3. It is especially important to teach parents to set emotional/financial/time limits with reinforcements, so that they are more likely to be able to follow through. If parents set up unrealistic expectations and then are unable to follow through with the reinforcement (i.e. Xbox or PlayStation) then consistency falls apart.

4. Teaching parents that reinforcement is not about just getting something, but that "earning" also gives you an opportunity to teach the life skill of work ethic. You do the very best job you possibly can, rather than the minimum amount necessary to earn a reinforcement.

Example 3: Punishment

"Why is it that my child doesn't care when I take stuff away from them?"

1. Every time your child misbehaves (regardless of the behavior) you take away telephone privileges. That child knows that they will eventually get the telephone back, making the punishment less meaningful. They are likely to return to the former behavior, because they do not recognize the punishment as a true loss. Loss of phone privileges can be much more meaningful if used for a negative communication behavior (i.e. screaming at a sibling, using foul language, gossiping), but far less meaningful for a behavior outside of the communication realm (i.e. stealing or breaking objects). Trying to match the loss with the initiating behavior makes for a more meaningful internal connection.

2. Physical punishment is not actually connected to a behavior, therefore making that type of punishment unmeaningful too. How many parents have spanked their children for misbehaving, only to have them do the same behavior three days later. This leads to the belief by parents that "nothing works." Often times, parents use physical punishment in response to physical aggression by children. This only sends a mixed message to kids in that we are essentially saying, "It's not okay for you to be aggressive, but it is okay for me to be aggressive."

3. Physical punishment, even when used minimally, increases aggressive behavior in children towards peers and adults. Often times, parents feel that the "quick fix" of spanking does the job in the moment, but in the long run it teaches children to respond to their environment and unexpected frustrations aggressively.

4. When I teach punishment to parents, we often attempt to add a paradoxical behavior that is an expectation of positive behavior, and a method of retraining for shaping. For example, "You just hit your brother, and that's not okay in our house. . .I want you to go and hug him and tell him that you love him." I also teach parents to add chore scheduling. For example, "Because you threw your toys and slammed your door, this week you have an extra job in the house of picking up in the living room and the bathroom every single day."

5. Punishment that is meaningful and directed at learning from your environment, rather than constant losses, can decrease co-morbid mood disturbance and issues with self-esteem and personal confidence building.

Example 4: Bribery

Bribery does not work. Many times parents and teachers consider reinforcement, "bribery." A distinction must be made between these two methods of interacting with children. Bribery means that you always give something *before* the behavior followed by the expectation that they will do what you want them to do. Reinforcement means that you always give them something *after* the behavior.

1. You are on trial for murder. You approached the judge to offer her $1 million for a "not guilty" finding. If you give the judge money before the trial, she is likely to find you "guilty" and walk away with your money, because she already has the money without the need for the behavior to occur. If you offer and show her that you have the money if she finds you "not guilty" then she is likely to find you "not guilty" out of desire to have the money.

2. You say "I'll pay you allowance if you do your chores." The child asks for an advance on the allowance and you give the money to them before the bedroom is cleaned up and the trash is taken out. They never finish the chores, because they already have what they wanted before having to follow the guidelines for the earned reinforcement.

Example 5: Defining what *"needs* to be done, rather than what does *not* need to be done"

As often as possible I attempt to teach parents and staff that when we tell children what *not* to do, then we have given them several loopholes in behavioral expectations. Children will perform a different behavior and say, "Well, you didn't tell me *not* to do that." Starting out as young as 2–3 years of age we want to change our language with kids to reflect our actual expectations, so there is no question about the expected behavior.

1. Instead of "stop running" you want to say "walk." If you tell them to stop running, then they have a tendency to roll down the hallway or weave back and forth between peers.

2. Instead of saying "stop jumping on the couch" you want to say "sit down." If you tell them to stop jumping, then they will roll or climb around the back of the couch or jump over to the coffee table because your request was not specific enough.

3. Instead of saying "stop screaming" you want to say "use your inside voice." If you tell them to stop screaming or cursing they will sing loudly, growl, or bark.

4. With teenagers, if you say "stop saying the F-word" instead of "please use kind words/appropriate language when you talk to me" they will simply choose another curse word to exchange.

Week 2

Personal De-Escalation and Prevention

The Importance of Self-Regulation

Parent's Personal Time-Out

Quiet Time

Learning to Recognize Escalation

Week 2

Parenting Skills Outline

Personal De-Escalation and Prevention

- Review use of "new skills" at home, including review of homework handouts and change in household structure. Validate and empower parents with troubleshooting. Allowing group discussion gives you an opportunity to have input as you moderate and point out missed steps or potential inconsistencies. Be careful not to invalidate parents that clearly did not participate in trying new skills. Allow them to process their thoughts about the new skills, even if they didn't try them because they were "too busy" or "forgot." Have extra handouts from the week before, so they can work on those with other parents present.

- Discussion of the brain and the need for **Self-Regulation**.

- Introduce the **"Parent's Personal Timeout"** (Effective with all adults)
  1. To be used to avoid disciplining when angry or frustrated
  2. Recognize the importance of this step to avoid unrealistic discipline, consequences, or reinforcement contingencies. (Example: "You are grounded for one year.") This technique teaches children, through modeling, that they are also able to take time away from high levels of emotion to avoid trouble or "saying something you don't mean."
  3. **Steps to Parent's Personal Timeout:**
     a. State to the child, *"I'm going to take a minute to calm down before I say something I don't mean. . .This doesn't mean you are getting out of it, I just need to take a short break."*
     b. Parent leaves the location of the child for deep breaths, a restroom break, walk, cigarette, etc. (Not intended to increase anger by mulling, but to "chill out.")
     c. Return to the child after a few minutes and state, *"I am glad that I took that time, because I was able to calm down when I was upset and think about what I really wanted to say to you."*
     d. Then discipline realistically.

- Introduce **"Quiet Time"**: The child's version of personal timeout (effective with all ages).
  1. This is a preventative opportunity for a child to calm and self-regulate *before* requiring cool-down or some form of responsive discipline.
  2. Help parents to be aware of children's behaviors as they escalate (escalatory cues):
     a. Can use the escalator metaphor.
     b. Can use the Anger Volcano metaphor. (The Anger Volcano Handout)
  3. Note that this is a technique to teach the skill of self-control to the child, and can help parents recognize their own shortfalls in areas of impulse control.

19

4. Rules and Steps to Quiet Time

    a. Not to be used if the child has acted out or been aggressive either physically or verbally. This technique is to be used before those behaviors occur.

    b. Identify the escalation without name-calling or labeling the child's behavior as "bad" or "negative." (You can start with statements of, "You seem like you're not feeling well right now" or "You seem like you're pretty upset right now.")

    c. Offer a quiet space or activity that does not promote increased aggressive behavior to prevent escalation from progressing.

        i. Effective Quiet Activities:

            1. Playing in bedroom with a toy that is <u>not</u> technology-based (i.e. first-person role-play games or aggressive video game play).

            2. Coloring or directed art activities.

            3. Reading comic books or books that are not schoolwork based.

            4. Playing calmly with a pet.

        ii. Ineffective Quiet Activities:

            1. Aggressive video games.

            2. Loud or angry music.

            3. Running outside.

            4. Punching a pillow or ripping paper (considered an aggressive exchange behavior which increases the likelihood of future aggression).

            5. Leaving the house with friends.

    d. Allow the child to remain in a quiet area as long as necessary to calm and self-regulate themselves.

    e. The child is to return when they are calm for praise ("It's good you were able to do that, because I know that sometimes it seems pretty hard to calm down when we get angry").

***Offer this as an option in the future with the parent as "a helper," if needed. Some parents say they don't think that it will work, but if you have them to try this for two weeks, and note differences in their home environment or their kid's interactions with other children, it can help them be more likely to approach preventative techniques, rather than being responsive to aggressive behaviors.

Week 2

Troubleshooting/Validation

The first activity the group participates in is troubleshooting and validating personal experiences of the homework from the week prior. We have a tendency to give people skills without following up, and then wonder why it is that they were unsuccessful or feel disempowered with the new parenting techniques. You must be sure they have the basic building blocks of the foundation in place, before moving on to more expansive skills. You will get questions about how to handle the child when they refused to go to cool-down time. I generally tell parents to give a choice to the child. For example, "If you stay in cool-down time then you can be finished with this and go play or call your friends. If you choose to keep getting out of this space then we will have to stay here until you are able to learn to sit." Remind them to tell the child that "cool-down time does not start until you sit down."

Emphasize the importance of being consistent, and not giving up on a skill after it doesn't work once. One of the failings of parenting skills training in the past is that we did not take time to focus on the normal resistance to changes in any given environment. You may want to discuss the 30-day improvement timeline that comes with consistent effort. It is important to identify that after week two of consistency, and what appears to be significant improvement, children often test limits (boundaries) and try to push parents out of using a new technique. They should expect positive and permanent changes (albeit more slowly than expected by some parents) beginning at about week three of the newly introduced tool, but especially after maintaining consistency for longer than 30 days.

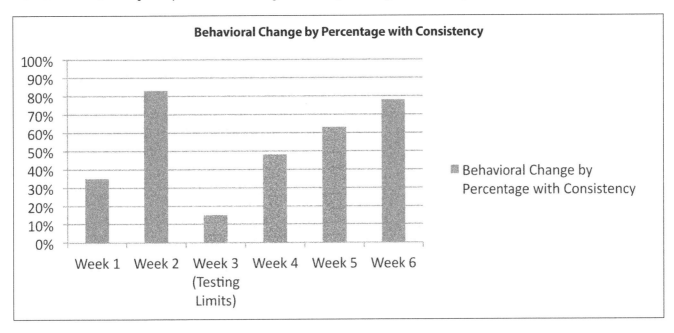

At this time in the group, I often discuss the way that the brain responds to environmental stimuli. We focus a lot of research attention on prefrontal cortex functioning in regards to decision-making and higher-order planning, but we fail to give attention to the autonomic nervous system. This area of the brain is our first responder when environmental stimuli become overwhelming. The way that I discuss the autonomic nervous system function is that "not all people run at a calm and collected internal baseline, which is when our thinking is relatively clear and our problem-solving

21

and processing is really working pretty well." For some individuals, they are constantly running at a high level of sensory engagement and over-sensitization to interactions with others. I try to challenge parents and staff to consider incorporating self-regulation activities into their daily routine. I request that parents incorporate activities such as deep breathing, systematic relaxation, prayer, mindfulness, and self-awareness activities at a minimum of five times each day. By incorporating these types of activities into your routine, you decrease the necessity to constantly be responding to negative or acting out behaviors as they are "nipped in the bud" *before* they have an opportunity to develop. By moving the sympathetic nervous system further away from threshold, which is the precipice to the fight or flight response, we actually increase one's likelihood of being able to process and engage with our environment in an effective and self-regulated way. By teaching the practice of **Parent's Personal Timeout** and **Quiet Time** for children, we offer opportunities throughout the day when we can consciously engage in self-regulation behaviors. When you advocate this as a practice for a family or a group of peers, we assist the entire milieu in becoming more regulated and less sensitive to environmental changes or unnecessary triggers for aggression.

In addition, parents and staff often fail to recognize that the intensity of their own emotions frequently get in the way of appropriate parenting and effective interactions with children. Using adult examples of unnecessarily escalated arguments or environmental responses can highlight the importance of learning to "calm down" *before* saying or doing something regretful or necessitating adult levels of discipline (i.e. write-ups at work, social avoidance, or police involvement within the marital home). Allow parents to discuss times when they have over or under-disciplined because they were not thinking clearly in times of anger or frustration. This is also an excellent opportunity to decrease the potential for child abuse. We discuss at length that some of our children's behaviors can be learned through observation of our own emotional difficulties and problems controlling aggression and agitation in their presence. By teaching prevention models, this gives adults and children alike an opportunity to calm down before "going off and having a consequence." The best way to teach children under the age of 12 is to lead by example. Children learn to generalize observed behaviors much more quickly than trained emotional control skills.

HOMEWORK WEEK 2: Practice Parents Personal Timeout, Quiet Time, and Self-Regulation Tools

Week #2

Handout for Parents

Steps to a Parent's Personal Timeout

1. Say to your child, "*I'm going to take a minute to calm down before I say something I don't mean. This doesn't mean that you are getting out of it, I just need a little break.*"

2. Leave the area for calming activities (whatever works for you, but be sure that you come back).

3. Return to your child and say, "*I am glad I took that time, because I was able to calm down and think about what I really wanted to say to you.*"

4. Discipline realistically.

Handout for Parents

Examples of Calming Activities

1. Go for a walk.

2. Wash dishes or do a chore.

3. Listen to calm music.

4. Pray.

5. Call a friend.

6. Take three deep breaths.

7. Drink a glass of cold water.

8. Lay on the bed and feel your body relaxing into the covers.

9. Smile in the mirror.

10. Listen to music.

***Everyone has different ways to calm and relax themselves, and sometimes exploring what works for you is the best way to be successful.**

Week #2

Handout for Parents

Examples of Self-Regulation Activities

1. **Deep breathing**–When you take deep breaths, it's important to sit quietly in a chair with your back to the back of the seat and your feet on the floor (or you can lie down on your back on the couch or floor). When you take breaths, breathe in deeply and feel your stomach move while inhaling. Hold this for three seconds, and then slowly release your breath. Some people whisper the word "breathe" while releasing the air.

2. **Guided imagery**–Close your eyes in a calm and quiet place (sometimes the bathroom is the best area). See the positive story of you talking calmly with your child in your head, almost like a movie. Anytime something negative wants to interfere, simply open your eyes, take a deep breath, and return to the story in your head where you are successful and your child hears what you say. Finish this movie in your head with a hug for your child.

3. **Systematic relaxation**–Again, do this activity in a quiet and peaceful place. Pay attention to different parts of your body, and tighten one muscle area at a time. Hold that for ten seconds tightly, take a deep breath, and then release the tightness in those muscles while you exhale. Start with the top of your head and work on at least six different areas of your body before you stop (neck, shoulders, hands, stomach, thighs, calves, toes).

Week #2

Handout for Parents

Steps to Child's Quiet Time

1. Always use *before* the child has become verbally or physically aggressive.

2. Say, "*You seem like you're not feeling well or upset.*"

3. Offer a quiet space and non-aggressive activity.

4. Let them stay in quiet time as long as they feel like they need it.

5. When they return say, "*It's good you were able to do that, because sometimes it's even hard for me to stop being angry.*"

6. Offer, "*You can do this again if you need it, and it's okay to ask for quiet time.*"

Handout for Parents

The Anger Volcano

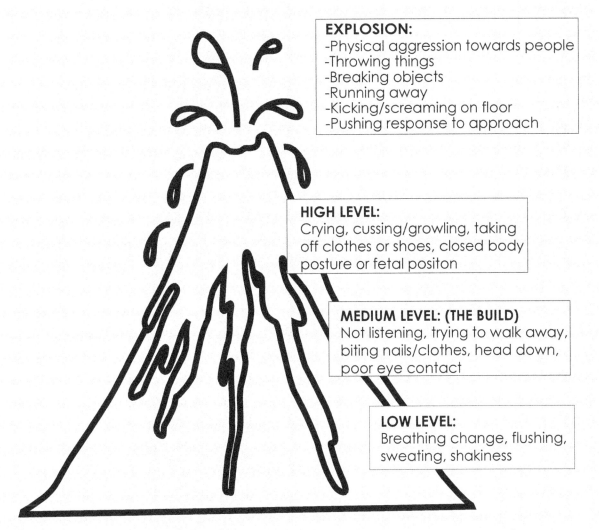

EXPLOSION:
-Physical aggression towards people
-Throwing things
-Breaking objects
-Running away
-Kicking/screaming on floor
-Pushing response to approach

HIGH LEVEL:
Crying, cussing/growling, taking off clothes or shoes, closed body posture or fetal positon

MEDIUM LEVEL: (THE BUILD)
Not listening, trying to walk away, biting nails/clothes, head down, poor eye contact

LOW LEVEL:
Breathing change, flushing, sweating, shakiness

What are the signs that my kid is getting ready to blow?
What do I look like when I am getting angry?

Week 2

Examples and Discussion Points

Example 1: Disciplining in Times of Anger

1. You are frustrated with your child for disobeying the rules at school and home (although discipline is best used in the place where the behavior happens in the first place—school at school and home at home). When you ask them why they did this, they say, "I don't know!" This makes you even more upset. You say, "You are grounded for a year!" Remember that you will have to be consistent, which means you are expected to actually ground them for one year. Who will have the longest year of their life? You! If you had taken the time to cool off by using a **personal timeout**, you could have prevented the misery of the next 365 days.

2. Many parents who use physical discipline often used this approach when they are angry with their child's behavior. Although we don't always mean to do that, we have a tendency to be more cruel and aggressive when angry, hurt, or frustrated with the situation. Physical abuse is a serious charge that can often be substantiated by a small bruise, red mark, or complaints of soreness by your child. If you physically punish when you're angry, it increases your chances of inflicting abuse on your child. It is a more worthwhile investment of your time to relax and cool off before you discipline, because it's not worth the removal of your child from your home or involvement with social services. Or better yet, is it worth the guilt you may feel if you do leave marks on your child? Unfortunately, this also teaches children to be aggressive when they are angry. When children see you being aggressive, although we are telling them not to be, this can be perceived as a one-way street. When you create confusion about different standards for behaviors, children have a tendency to do what they see rather than what they are told.

Example 2: The Escalator

The escalator is an excellent visual reference that most parents can understand to describe the increase in aggression or anger. The escalator moves slowly in an upward direction, just as our emotions do. At the bottom of the escalator you have a choice whether to step on or step off. Once you're on the escalator it is difficult to get off, because it works against you as you turn and attempt to walk downward (increasing frustration). Imagine each moving step as a step closer to acting out. Many of us can watch our children (and honestly ourselves) "work themselves up" or escalate into a frenzy of bad behavior. At the top, we can get caught in a group of people or have to wait in line to return to the bottom. In the meantime, we are getting into trouble or hurting ourselves in the fight to de-escalate.

Example 3: The Anger Volcano

The Anger Volcano (handout) is also an excellent visual cue for understanding escalatory behaviors, which have potential to be defused before explosion. Volcanoes essentially tell us when they're getting ready to explode or erupt, by doing things like grumbling, shaking, steaming, or making noises (not unlike our children). If we do not pay attention to the warning signs, it is more likely for the things around the volcano to be destroyed after explosion. If we take the time to recognize those early warning signs, an alarm system of sorts, it gives us an opportunity to intervene before the explosion (i.e. assistance with self-regulation/coping skill behaviors) and we can actually prevent the severity of the damage to the surrounding area from the volcano (i.e. relationships, property, self-esteem).

Week 3

Cycles

Emotion Cycles
Using Diffusing Techniques
Understanding How Technology Sensitizes

Week 3

Parenting Skills Outline

Cycles

- Review use of "new skills" at home, including review of homework handouts and change in response to **Self-Regulation, Personal Timeouts,** and **Quiet Time**. Validate and empower parents with troubleshooting.

- Revisit the importance of consistency and following through while highlighting the notion of "choosing your battles wisely."

  i. Allow parents to ask themselves, *"Am I investing emotional time and energy in an argument that could be better used elsewhere?"*

- Introduce "**Cycles**"

  1. All behaviors, thoughts, and emotions occur in cycles.

  2. Everything we say or do has some type of impact on our immediate surroundings and world (can use the visual aid of the circle with arrows equaling meltdown or "explosion").

  3. Every emotion can be tied to an external trigger or experience.

     a. Triggers (antecedents) are unable to be reversed or "taken back" once it has been initiated (e.g. pulling the trigger on a gun).

     b. Allow parents to explore what types of things cause their own emotional responses.

        i. Anger- Being told to do something you don't want to do.

        ii. Sadness- Being made fun of or talked down to.

        iii. Happiness- Being praised or told you are important.

        iv. Frustration- Being given criticism in the work place.

  4. Use of the washing machine metaphor to illustrate how anger cycles are triggered, as well as opportunities for pulling out of cycles.

  5. How can you pull out of the cycle? (With coping and diffusing techniques)

     a. Use of "apology" to defuse the trigger, which is not an apology for the discipline itself, but for perhaps a feeling created within the child.

     b. Practicing "I" statements and paraphrasing to allow children to feel validated by matching the perception of the current incident for the parent and child (Handout).

     c. Use of Personal Timeouts and Quiet Area to decrease the intensity of the cycle.

     d. Other *individualized* coping skills.

    6. Be sure to use adult examples that can apply to parent's interpersonal relationships either with their spouse or in occupational relationships.

- Discussion of the impact of technology on brain function and how it can often be an unidentified **trigger** to initiate a cycle.

    1. Removing technology from the bedroom, homework areas, and dinner table:

        a. Decreases the likelihood of over-sensitization to environmental triggers (i.e. the unexpected explosion).

        b. Increases the brain's ability to focus on interactions with others, and processing.

        c. Increases opportunities for direct one-on-one engagement when attempting to initiate new parenting/staff techniques.

Week 3

Troubleshooting/Validation

During this week's session it is vital to review parents' ability to calm themselves before disciplining. It is important to point out subtle differences and nuances in temperament, and how these changes can increase the parents' ability to impact their children in a positive way. You will find that by week three, parents are using concepts of reinforcement much more frequently, and appropriately, than punishment. Assist parents in identifying their own specific experiences of compliance and reference their own mood during these interactions with their child.

This week's session focuses on the concept of emotional cycles. This topic begins to illustrate to parents that even small changes in language, body posturing/nonverbal cues, and verbal communication can affect how their children respond in a positive way. The concept of cycles also gives the group an opportunity to understand their own accountability, and establish a sense of personal responsibility for triggering behaviors, rather than identifying their child's behavior as "only their problem." The use of metaphor is an effective method of teaching this concept, and I often use the imagery of the washing machine to teach parents how it is possible to pull children out of cycles even if they were unintentionally triggered.

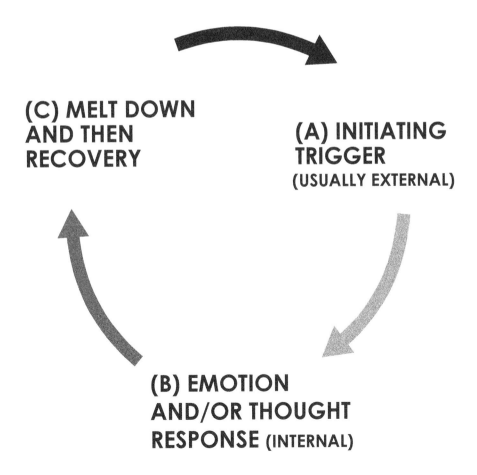

(C) MELT DOWN AND THEN RECOVERY

(A) INITIATING TRIGGER (USUALLY EXTERNAL)

(B) EMOTION AND/OR THOUGHT RESPONSE (INTERNAL)

When discussing the concept of triggers/antecedents: (A) It is important to note that triggers can be verbal, physical, and non-verbal. (When working with ASD populations, at times triggers have been present long before initiation from another person. For example, hypersensitivity to environmental stimuli.) Generally, people initiate cycles of emotions through non-verbal communication and verbal cues before ever being triggered by physical cues (except in cases of persistent physical threat, harm, or abuse). Helping parents and teachers recognize that the tone, tempo, and timing of their commentary can lead to escalation, is a good first step in helping adults comprehend how they impact the child and others. Sometimes, simply by increasing this awareness you are able to decrease unnecessary triggers.

When identifying emotional responses, (B) help parents understand that just because they exhibit anger, sadness, and frustration in certain ways does not mean that their children respond in a like fashion. Often children do not become overt with their emotional response until they are near to the point of "meltdown." Therefore, it is helpful to give parents time to reflect on cues their children are identifying before full escalation (e.g. social withdrawal, decreased eye contact, changes in breathing patterns, refusal to speak, etc.)

This is the time in group where we return to the imagery of the "anger volcano" and the worksheet provided in the week previously. By having awareness of the imagery of the anger volcano, they can begin to recognize the concept of escalation in reference to triggered cycles. Not only do we want to increase the awareness of the escalation, but during this week we attempt to focus on the possibility of not initiating the escalation in the first place by altering the antecedents (please use the term "word trigger" as it is easier for parents to comprehend and apply outside of the group setting).

After you have discussed the concept of cycles and offer parents an opportunity to identify their own examples (either with their own children or in occupational/family interactions) it is important to discuss healthy ways to assist in de-escalation from an already triggered cycle. Remember that the idea is to explore effective coping skills, not "*coping skills, schmoping skills.*"

One generally effective verbal coping skill, or pull out technique, is an apology. Be careful when discussing this concept, because many parents have the tendency to feel the need to apologize for the discipline itself. We want to emphasize the importance of being consistent, and that we don't want them to lose their parental power by backing out of appropriate disciplinary techniques. Rather, we want to allow parents to recognize that we are apologizing for the impact on their child's emotions (we are teaching them to validate their children). Parents already know from week two that they need to calm themselves before interacting with their child in the role of limit-setter, so there should be far fewer incidents of improper or unrealistic discipline. Therefore, when apologies are made early in the initiated cycle, they should sound like, "I'm sorry you are feeling angry right now" or "I'm sorry you feel like I tried to hurt your feelings on purpose." Again, reviewing the importance of less threatening "I" statements is an effective method of communicating with our children so that they feel validated and engaged with parents.

Other coping skills you may want to introduce to parents:

1. Take 2–3 steps away from each other (decreasing proximity). Techniques of decreasing intensity of proximity often assist in de-escalating triggered cycles. This also holds true in academic and residential settings, where the tendency of staff is to approach an aggressive behavior rather than step away and give it space to "fizzle-out."

2. Smile and continue to make positive/calm eye contact (positive non-verbal cueing). Sometimes the use of paradoxical (the opposite of the presented emotion) facial expressions can actually change the limbic system response to the engagement, and decrease aggression.

3. Sit on the floor and take deep breaths (modeling self-regulation). In "the heat of the moment" the very best approach you can take is to decrease verbal interaction, which disengages the sympathetic nervous system and initiates the parasympathetic nervous system to calm the internal response to cues. By modeling these behaviors during that time, you allow children to observe others practicing coping mechanisms that can be just as effective for them in that moment.

4. Selective ignoring (removal of negative attention/reinforcer). I teach parents daily this notion of ignoring behaviors they do not want to reinforce or increase in presentation (extinguishing negative behaviors). When we teach selective ignoring, we are not teaching parents to ignore aggressive or physically threatening/harmful behaviors. We are teaching them to defuse anger by not giving it attention through eye contact, proximity, verbal address, or physical contact.

Another area of parenting that **must** respond to social change is the idea of excessive exposure to technology and how it has an impact on our brain's ability to regulate. What we often fail to recognize is that this kind of unneeded exposure to technological stimulation preemptively elevates our internal sensitivity, before we even add environmental impact or other triggers. We are surrounded by technology constantly, whether it be our "smart" phones, tablets, PCs, video games, or television sets; not just at home, but in public places and even our school classrooms. Research has shown is that excessive exposure to technology has an impact on prefrontal cortex development, limbic system response to environmental cues, and temporal lobe development. During this week, I attempt to promote the removal of unnecessary technology in bedrooms, homework areas, at the dinner table, and when it is unnecessary to use in classrooms.

Especially in the bedroom, we want to decrease technological exposure to assist with having an area of calm without excessive sensory stimuli. I have parents that say, "They cannot sleep without the television set on, what do you want me to do about that?" My response to that question is often that we have created a need for that type of engagement at bedtime, which has a negative impact on establishing regular circadian rhythm and effective sleep patterns. I want to validate parents and their frustration with an expectation such as removing something that has been there "since they were a small child."

One technique we use to decrease the need for television exposure at night is to wean exposure. In the first week, we decrease the volume of the television each night, and include the use of a timer for shut off (if available on the television set). In the following week, we will place a bathroom towel or tea towel over the screen, so as not to have flickering lights and unnecessary visual engagement when attempting to initiate sleep. By the third week, we decrease the amount of exposure time by more than 70%, and this is when we discover that children sleep more effectively. By having children that are better rested they also are less likely to have aggressive responses and oversensitivity to environmental stimuli.

Having technology in homework areas and at the dinner table, only serves as a distraction and one extra environmental trigger that is unnecessarily sensitizing the internal cycle. We work with families to understand the importance of not having television sets, radios, computers, or video games on during homework time. By doing this, we increase the likelihood of task-focus and decrease the necessity for arguments about failure to complete assignments or poor work quality. At the dinner table, we focus on the importance of face-to-face interactions between parents and children, to increase the likelihood of sharing current experiences and allow children and parents to feel validated in their interactions.

HOMEWORK WEEK 3: Practice the identification of cycles and triggers for the next week, attempt to use functional coping mechanisms to "pull out" of cycles before meltdown, and decrease exposure to technology in the home.

Week #3

Handout for Parents

How to use "I" Statements and Paraphrasing

From your child:

1. Their body temperature is up, face is red, and they refuse to make eye contact.

2. They start to stomp their feet, they say "I hate you," and tell you to leave them alone.

3. They curse you and tell you that you are a terrible parent.

4. They tell you that your rules are stupid.

What you can say:

1. "I see that you feel angry right now."

2. "I'm sorry that made you feel upset, but I always love you no matter what."

3. "I see that you are really angry, but I'm trying the best I can."

4. "Sometimes I don't like the rules either, but I still have to follow them."

Paraphrasing: Repeating what you think you have heard without using the same words (can be perceived as mocking), but touching on the key points of the communication.

Handout for Parents

The Washing Machine and Pulling Out of Cycles

- The laundry is ruined
- The most difficult time to pull-out
- When the most damage is likely to happen
- This is the time a consequence or discipline happens

- Turning "on" the washing machine
- The Trigger (can't be taken back)
- Words
- A look
- Expectations
- Stress

Meltdown **Calm**

Emotion or Thought **Physical**

- You go to put in the fabric softener and see the pen
- Excellent time to move away
- Selective ignoring

- The ink pen is floating
- Perfect time for an apology
- Opportunity to paraphrase the feeling being shown by their body.

Week 3

Examples and Discussion Points

Example 1: The Washing Machine

What do you have in your home that has a cycle? A washing machine.

Your washing machine has several settings on it, but the ultimate goal is to have clean clothes in the end. Imagine if you set your washing machine to clean "whites" and you didn't realize that there was an ink pen in the water. What would happen to your load of laundry? Your clothes would be ruined (can equate with the meltdown for children, because it takes a lot of effort to clean up the mess that results). If you could get the pen out of the washing machine before it ruined everything, then you would be preventing a huge mess (meltdown). You have many options to remove the pen before it damages all the items of clothing. The best would be not to have the pen in the washing machine in the first place, but if you saw it floating on top of the water when you filled it, then you could pull the pen out without too much hassle. If you couldn't get the pen at that time, perhaps you see it floating when you go to put the fabric softener into the load. At that time, you could pull the pen out with only minor damage (during escalation). If you allow the cycle to complete, there is little that you can do to manage the damage.

This metaphor is not unlike anger (emotion) cycles. A trigger is the starting point (when you turn the washing machine on) and the opportunity to remove the impact of the trigger (pulling the pen out). This is the time you have an opportunity to utilize a *functional* coping skill to pull out of the cycle. Parents enjoy this example, because it is visual and they can comprehend the information, rather than speaking the jargon of triggers/antecedents, coping skills, etc.

Example 2: Alarm Makes You Late for Work

This is a good example for parents in assisting them to understand that they too have cycles of anger and emotions. It helps them to recognize that anger is a normal emotion, but it is what you do with the anger that sets you aside from others, and can either cause problems or allow an opportunity for regulation.

You wake up late, because you set the alarm for PM not AM. You run out of hot water in the shower, because everyone else in the house showered first. The car started without trouble, but you get stuck behind a school bus on your way to work. When you finally get around the bus you race to work "only 15 minutes late." Before you turn at your work entrance, a police officer pulls you over for speeding (perfect!). You're now 45 minutes late to work and your anger cycle was initiated (triggered) over an hour ago. As you enter the workplace your boss makes a comment that your pay will be docked for the tardiness. This is the point in your cycle that is the most difficult to pull out of, as it has been building for quite some time. It would have served you better to have called in to say that you were going to be late to begin with, rather than rushing and escalating the cycle. In response to your boss's comment you scream, yell, and tell him exactly where to put his job. The consequences to that meltdown are quite likely getting fired or a loss of income. Where do you think you could have pulled out of your cycle with a healthy coping skill in order to avoid the mess you are now in?

Changing How We Communicate with Each Other

Changing Communication
Removing Unneeded Word Triggers
Facilitating Smooth Transitions
Creating Internal Organization

Week 4

Parenting Skills Outline

Changing How We Communicate with Each Other

- Review use of "new skills" at home, including review of homework handouts and change in response with use of **pulling out of cycles**. Validate and empower parents with troubleshooting.

- **Introduce "Verbal Antecedents/Word Triggers"** (effective with all ages)

  1. Words are usually the first initiator of unneeded escalation cycles (primary trigger).

  2. What kinds of things set our kids off more than anything else?

     a. Hearing the word "no."

     b. Having adults make requests for behaviors.

     c. Being overwhelmed by list of expectations that are verbally driven.

  3. Children don't usually come out of the box punching (within immediate physical aggression). Usually they can be seen escalating with verbal aggression, excessive mouth noises, growling, grunting, or other language cues. We need to start with language to prevent further escalation.

- **Identify problems within households/classrooms with verbal triggers or escalated interactions**

  1. Usually begins with arguments immediately following school and/or work.

     a. Establish with parents the importance of free-time each day after school.

        i. Many children have worked a ten-hour day (from the time they wake up and step onto the school bus until the time they come home) and need an opportunity to rest and recover before starting homework or chores.

        ii. Children are most fatigued and lacking in attention in the afternoon hours.

     b. Help parents remember that they are now able to identify when their children are escalating.

  2. You will hear: "My kid overreacts to *everything* that comes out of my mouth."

     a. Identify and discuss communication trends within the home.

     b. Question parents regarding the communication style of school staff.

        i. For example, do they feel overwhelmed when they attend school meetings themselves?

     c. Identify what types of language they feel is appropriate in the presence of their children.

        i. Foul language

        ii. Name-calling

        iii. Strong emotional language

        iv. Bad mouthing school staff, family members, or supervisors

        v. Bad mouthing spouses during separation or divorce

   d. Discuss what is, and what is not, appropriate to communicate to and in the presence of your children.

        i. Remember that children will do and say as you do and say.

        ii. You are their primary model for appropriate language.

        iii. If you teach them not to say and do things, but do them yourself, you are sending a mixed message, which can be confusing for social and emotional development.

   e. Identify potential triggers/verbal antecedents for cycle initiation. (Again, words are usually the first trigger in emotive cycles)

- **Three Methods of Avoiding and Altering Verbal Antecedents/Word Triggers:** Assist parents in adjusting their own communication style, while also reflecting on how they feel/perceive it when other people use these unintentional word triggers on them.

   1. *Don't ever ask a question that you already know the answer to.*

      a. When you do this, you often set your children up for lying or manipulation to avoid consequence.

        i. "Did you clean your room yet?"

        ii. "Did you get in trouble at school today?"

        iii. "Is your homework done?"

      b. Always state directly, as asking a question you already know the answer to is passive-aggressive and teaches children to do so with others.

   2. *Do not make requests for behaviors when your child is obviously irritable, upset, or otherwise involved in an activity.*

      a. Introduce the concept of "priming the pump" for expected transitions.

      b. Counting with the numbers "1, 2, 3" can be a nice auditory cue to prepare children for requested expectations before the shift.

      c. Be sure to establish appropriate eye contact, but be cautious not to expect extended eye contact because this can be distracting for children.

      d. Have them repeat your request in their own words to assure that not only are you giving a directive, but they are able to process and comprehend the expectation.

   3. *Do not make run-on verbal lists for children's behaviors.*

      a. Introduce the concept of visual cueing for chore lists and household expectations (you can bring magazines and paper into group to create chore lists that parents are able to use immediately in the home).

      b. Query parents when they have finished their own list of skills to learn for group on that day, "Doesn't it feel good when you finish a list?"

      c. Identify the appropriate number of chores or expectations for different age groups.

        i. Two to three regular responsibilities each day for children younger than eight (be sure you don't ask them to clean their room, the kitchen, and the bathroom, as that is a masked list of 57 responsibilities).

        ii. Five to seven regular responsibilities for kids eight to 18.

        iii. Be aware of your child's developmental or cognitive limitations before assigning responsibilities.

Week 4

Troubleshooting/Validation

Generally, this tends to be the week when even you're most resistant and angry parents/staff make a turnaround. This is the week when you start seeing "lights turn on" for many parents that are truly attempting to use their new skills within their homes, and returning with questions for troubleshooting. This will only happen if you as a clinician or teacher have maintained a non-judgmental atmosphere with open communication and creative solution development. I still find it amazing to watch parents entering their fourth week with their bells ringing and excitement in their faces. Prepare yourself for increasingly specific questions during this and following sessions. If you don't know an answer to a specific question, never be afraid to say, "I don't know." I always make sure I follow up a statement like that with, "I will find you an answer before you come back next week."

By this time, many of the group participants are beginning to recognize that what they say and how they behave in front of their children has made a determined impact on their child's behavior. Important areas to explore, and also the most sensitive of topics, are:

1. Persistent adult arguing within the home.

2. Argument styles of different parents or family members, which are often well-modeled to children, and observable in school settings and social interactions with other children.

3. Discussion and recognition of persistent communication difficulties with the school, court, or social services system.

Taking the time to identify each of these problems for the parents attending group allows them to identify their own cycled behaviors, and develop awareness and empathetic responses to their children's frustrations. I have parents say, "I didn't even realize that my kids felt exactly the same way I did. How did I miss that?" I validate these feelings for parents, as well as help them to recognize that when you're living in the moment or in the "feeling that is happening at the time" it's often very difficult to recognize similarities with others. These types of negative interactions and communication styles with others often leave us feeling isolated and as if we are failures. If we can help parents understand these concepts at this point in group, we can also help increase their ability to be present with their children's frustrations.

Of utmost importance is the analysis and gentle changing of the language used (content and context) within the home. Helping parents become aware that whatever comes out of their mouths will likely be repeated by their children, regardless of the context, will have a long-term impact on the household and family structure, as well as their children's ability to function outside of the home. For example, foul language, prejudicial comments, and negative feelings voiced toward school staff or social services will affect whether children are able to appropriately interact with similar people. I frequently emphasize that what occurs between adults (e.g. IEP meetings, placement planning, disagreements about interventions, arguments about parenting style, and visitation planning) should stay between adults. Children already hear far too much adult information as it is, and technology has not helped limit that exposure whatsoever. If these kinds of "adult" conversations are openly addressed with children present, it can lead to difficulties comprehending their roles as children in these environments, and recognizing appropriate verbal boundaries with adults and authority figures. This is a nice time to reflect on what types of adult language the parenting group was raised with, and how this has impacted their own ability to function occupationally or socially.

Help parents understand that while it is perfectly normal for them to not get along with everyone in their child's life, their children do not have a choice of walking away from those interactions as an adult would. Essentially, do not create confusion for your children. For example, children must return to school each day and comply with rules and expectations given by their teachers. Regardless of how their parents feel about that individual, assignments and course participation *must* be completed. What children think is, "I am supposed to do what my teacher says, but my mom hates her so why should I even bother?" We don't want to create a "them vs. us" mentality, because this can cause long-term academic engagement and compliance issues for children.

Revisit cycles briefly and identify that the best-case scenario is to actually prevent the cycle from being initiated in the first place. The first trigger for cycles often is the words that we use and the language that is around us. So, how better to prevent escalation than to change the way that we communicate with our children. There are three simple rules to altering or avoiding unneeded verbal antecedents (word triggers), and in return we can decrease the frequency of escalations and unneeded explosions in the home:

1. **The first rule for altering verbal antecedents: Don't ever ask a question you already know the answer to.** As adults we have a tendency to ask the questions that we know the answers to in an effort to motivate others to comply with our wishes. This is a passive-aggressive approach to interacting with others, and often leads to unnecessary escalation. This change is basically teaching parents and children common courtesy, and through modeling and learned behavior you can successfully develop those skills. We adults feel condescended towards when someone asks this kind of question. You may have even had this experience with a supervisor or colleague when they approach you and say, "Did you get that work done yet?" They know full well that your work is piled up on your desk, and you probably have not finished it. This only serves to agitate and engage internal negative thoughts and emotions that are likely to result in explosion, or at least initiated agitation. Even in our own interpersonal relationships we do this. For example, asking your spouse "Did you get the oil changed in the car?" Despite the fact that the motor exploded on the way to work after the check-engine light came on. Adults have more of a tendency to communicate this way with children, as we feel that asking questions is a motivator. During my seminars, I discuss the frequency of behaviors, such as having a parent walk by their child's mess of a room and then approaching them while the kid is watching television to ask "Did you clean your room yet?" Or perhaps, after a parent receives a phone call from school about their child fighting and having consequences they approach their child immediately and say, "Did you have any problems at school today?" This method of communicating is not only rude, but it sets children up for deceit and manipulation. Then they are being disciplined for not following through with the behavioral expectation, and they have another disciplinary action in reaction to dishonesty (e.g. "Yes, I cleaned my room" or "No, I had no problems at school"). It is best to be direct, and teach those communication skills to our children in their interactions with others.

Parents and teachers often don't realize that they are setting up a system of failure within their homes and school systems. By being honest and straightforward with children they will learn to do the same with others. No more tricky "Aha, I caught you in a lie! I can always count on you to lie about the smallest of things" (even though you set them up for it). Of course they lied. Either they don't want to get in trouble for not completing an expectation in the first place, or they have no idea what was said to them (because they were distracted) and they simply responded to your non-verbal cues of smiling while you ask the question.

2. **The second rule for altering verbal antecedents: Do not ask children to do something when they are obviously irritable, agitated, or otherwise occupied with an activity.** This is a basic cognitive behavioral intervention that allows us to assist with appropriate transition from one structured or unstructured activity to another. I hear complaint after complaint in my office regarding children who are "struggling with transition." The issue is not necessarily with their response to the transition, it is with the way that we are attempting to move them from one task to another (unless we are working with ASD populations, who are generally sensitive to unexpected change). We have this tendency to request children to immediately comply with requests, while they are busy playing a video game and haven't made it to a save area, or they are engaged in a television program or telephone conversation. And then we wonder why children constantly interrupt parents while they are speaking on the telephone, or teachers while they are instructing a classroom. We do exactly the same thing to them when we

have an expectation for a behavioral shift. They learn this from adults in their lives. With children, this type of interaction is even more of an issue, because if they are involved in another activity their concentration is not focused on the adult's request. Especially in the case of children that have issues with inattention or transitional shifting (i.e. ADHD and ASD populations), they will likely not even process the information, let alone be able to follow through with the expected shift. I teach **Priming the Pump** as an opportunity for successfully transitioning from one activity to another. By practicing this tool on a daily basis in our schools and homes we can potentially save hours of argument over simple requests like "You need to come to the dinner table" or "You don't have the right book in front of you. I told the whole class already."

A. The mentality behind **Priming the Pump**: Not unlike pumping water from an outside well. The first pump: Nothing happens. The second pump: A little bit of water flows. The third pump: That's when things start to happen.

   i. Our brains were not meant to suddenly shift from one activity to another.

   ii. Research on attention and shifting attention has clearly shown us that we require time to transition and refocus our energy on alternate tasks.

   iii. Children especially have difficulty transitioning from an unstructured to a structured activity.

   iv. By taking less than 3 minutes to "prime the cognitive pump" you can assist children with internal processing, time management, behavioral organization, and successful completion of step-by-step directives.

B. The steps to utilizing/practicing **Priming the Pump**: We make an effort to prime the cognitive pump three times. The first pump is a statement of intent, the second pump is a reminder of the expectation, and the third pump is an opportunity to follow through with the transition.

   i. **Pump 1:**

      a. Take a moment to verbally cue your child during a time where the activity they are participating in is at a lull (i.e. commercial break from television program) approximately five to ten minutes prior to the expected behavioral transition.

      b. Request eye contact to engage the brain and focus. Be especially cautious with children with ADHD symptoms that you do not request extended eye contact, as they are using most of their energy to focus on the maintenance of the eye contact instead of processing your verbal directive.

      c. State the expected shift to your child. For example, "In five minutes, I need you to turn off the television and come to the dinner table."

      d. Take the five seconds to request that the child repeat the expected behavior, and clarify any missed information. This allows children to not just cognitively process the expectation but associate language with the behavioral transition.

      e. Allow them to return to their activity without interruption.

   ii. **Pump 2:**

      a. Three to five minutes prior to the expected shift, again initiate contact by addressing them by name and requesting brief eye contact for engagement.

      b. State the expected shift to your child again. For example, "Don't forget, in three minutes, I need you to turn off the television and come to the dinner table."

      c. Allow them to verbally repeat the expectation.

      d. Allow them to return to the activity without interruption.

    iii. Pump 3:

      a. At the time of the expected transition, again address your child by name and requested eye contact.

      b. State (don't ask), "Now is the time you need to turn off the TV and come to the dinner table."

      c. Do not walk away from your child at that time, but assist them in understanding that you are there to help them with the transition.

      d. Do not have an expectation that they will do something other than your request (i.e. pick up their dirty dishes, put their socks in the laundry basket, or put away their video game player).

Parents often complain that this process seems a bit involved, but it is always important to reference the amount of time they are currently using to manage escalation related to a transition that hasn't been followed through upon request. By discussing the investment of less than the three minutes it takes to complete this activity, you often engage parents in being motivated to give it a chance. We will also practice this directly in parenting class as we transition for restroom breaks or are preparing to end class. It is also important to note, that depending upon the child's mood and demeanor at the time of the request, it is possible to remove the repetition component from the second request to avoid triggering a cycle due to agitation.

    The other thing that I have added to this technique is the use of visual cues for transition. For smaller children, we have often used stickers on the top of the hand as each pump occurs to allow for a visually paired cue with a verbal directive. In our school systems, we use visual boxes at the front of the room and a check mark after each pump to communicate to the entire classroom that an expected behavioral shift is coming. Some of my classroom teachers in Head Start and daycare facilities also use a stoplight, and pair the red light with pump one, the yellow light with pump two, and the green light with pump three (which tells us it's time to 'go'). Again, I have a strong preference for using visually and verbally paired cues, as I know that this has a tremendous impact on prefrontal cortex development and our ability to understand expectation for transition in our environment.

    3. The third rule for altering verbal antecedents: Don't make a run-on verbal list for your children to comply to. A good rule of thumb is that children under the age of 8 should have no more than three chores or behavioral expectations each day. Yes, children as young as 2 to 3 years old are perfectly capable of picking up their own toys, placing their dirty clothes in a basket, or putting books back onto a shelf. From age eight until 18 years old I request parents limit chore and behavioral expectations to no more than five to seven each day. The level of difficulty can be adjusted according to age and ability. Teaching the use of visual chore lists as non-verbal cues for expectation, rather than overwhelming children with a verbal list of expectations, gives children an opportunity to visually process and understand the expectation from their environment. Without the use of visually cued lists, we will continue to have children that are confused and will say to you "You never told me I needed to do that" even though you have already told them verbally 12 times. Many of the children that we work with have significant difficulty with auditory and verbal processing issues. If we simply verbally request an expectation, we are not allowing their brains to develop prefrontal cortex function of higher order thinking and organization, or left temporal lobe language sites. I gather the oldest magazines from my lobby (or second hand stores) and bring them into parenting class to cut and paste pictures of laundry baskets, dishes, clothes, or shoes for creating a visual checklist that can be photocopied and used in the home each day. I emphasize the importance of having a "fresh, clean list every single day" to allow children to feel a sense of accomplishment as they mark their completed activities off of the list. Even older adolescents benefit from the experience of "seeing" at least one thing through to completion each day. I also recommend to parents that nothing gets marked off of the list until the child has done "their best job possible." If we allow children to mark off activities that they have minimally performed, we are teaching them that is an effective way to live in our occupational world in the future. We want to teach work ethic by allowing children to remove the item from the list only when they've done the very best job possible, and you have checked it (and praised them for a good job done). Also, do not send mixed messages to your children by telling them it's okay to mark the task off of their list, and then leaning over and redoing the behavior (i.e. bed making, dishwashing, or organizing the magazines on the coffee table). What you are saying is, "Yeah, that might be okay, but I do it better."

For parents with children with developmental delays or processing issues, be sure that you personally assist them in choosing responsibilities that they are capable of completing. The idea is not to create a sense of disempowerment, but to give children a feeling of accomplishment and develop personal autonomy.

During this week, I also clearly explain the importance of children having "down time" after they return home from school each day. We discuss the importance of free time after returning from school to recover from the responsibilities of their taxing day. We want to allow them to rest, eat, and play prior to completing activities such as homework or chores. I have some doctors that say "make them sit down and do their homework right away, because that's when their medications are still working." Especially for ADHD populations, this may be true, but frustration tolerance levels and quality of work are extremely low late in the afternoon. What I have seen is that most stimulant medications have ceased to be therapeutically effective around approximately 3:00 PM or 4:00 PM in the afternoon. Offering those children an opportunity to move freely about and rest prior to an expected behavior can help them feel advocated for by their parents.

HOMEWORK WEEK 4: Increase Personal Awareness of How Parents/Staff Communicate in the Presence Children and Practice the 3 Steps to Avoiding or Altering Word Triggers.

Week #4

Handout for Parents

Priming the Pump

Pump One:

1. 5 to 10 minutes before you want your child to do something (wait for a commercial break from television programs, or save zones in video games).

2. Say their name and get their eyes to look at you briefly.

3. Tell them what change is coming.

4. Have them repeat what you said, and clear up any mistakes (give them a sticker so they can "see the first pump").

5. Walk away.

Pump Two:

1. 3 to 5 minutes before the change.

2. Say their name and get their eyes to look at you.

3. Tell them again what change is coming.

4. Have them repeat what you said, and clear up any mistakes (give them a sticker so they can "see the second pump").

5. Walk away.

Pump Three:

1. At the time of the change (move to the dinner table, get off the phone, turn off the video games, etc.).

2. Say their name and get their eyes to look at you.

3. Tell them "Now it's time to move" to the next thing (use the last sticker for pump three).

4. Stay with them, so they have help the first few times.

REPEAT, REPEAT, REPEAT

Week #4

Handout for Parents

List making for 3 to 8 years old:

These are your jobs for this week:

1. Put your clothes in the laundry basket.

2. Put your books back on the shelf.

3. Put your dishes in the sink.

Week #4

Handout for Parents

List making for 8 to 12 years:

These are your jobs for this week:

1.   Take out the garbage.

2.   Sweep the living room and hallway.

3.   Put away the washed dishes.

4.   Make your bed.

5.   Hang up your book bag and coat.

Week 4

Examples and Discussion Points

Example 1: Children Follow the Leader

This example is important for helping parents understand that their children do what they teach them to do through observed behavior, regardless of its level of appropriateness. Many parents don't even realize that their children are acting just as they do, or saying the same words that they are saying.

Do you remember the first word your child said? It is likely that they said that word because you stood in front of them for hours at a time saying "Mama" or "Daddy." *Follow the leader.* Do you remember your child trying to wipe the table at age four because they want to be just like you, and had carefully watched you wipe the table after dinner? *Follow the leader.* Do you remember when your child decided to sneak a cigarette, because even though they watched you cough and choke they wanted to be just like you? *Follow the leader.* Do you remember that they hit/yelled at that kid at school and got suspended, because even though you tell them to behave themselves, you have had physical/verbal fights with other people at the grocery store or in the hallway at school? *Follow the leader.* Do you remember the first time you got a call home from daycare or from the school because your child dropped the F-bomb or the S-word while they were playing with other kids on the playground? *Follow the leader.*

The list could go on and on with how children repeat exactly what they've heard, and participate in play-acting behaviors that they have seen. Help this apply specifically to the problems of your parents in group, and ask them for examples of either funny or uncomfortable moments when they heard their children say exactly what they have said in the most unexpected places. This is an opportunity to engage humor as part of group, and many parents have quite funny stories to share. By engaging humor, you also soothe the parents' brains (amygdala function) through the process of laughter and neurochemical change, while making internal connections for the memory of teaching the skill.

Example 2: Altering Verbal Antecedents

How to we change our language within the guidelines for altering verbal antecedents (word triggers)?

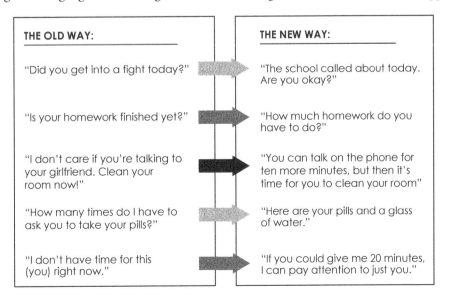

THE OLD WAY:	THE NEW WAY:
"Did you get into a fight today?"	"The school called about today. Are you okay?"
"Is your homework finished yet?"	"How much homework do you have to do?"
"I don't care if you're talking to your girlfriend. Clean your room now!"	"You can talk on the phone for ten more minutes, but then it's time for you to clean your room"
"How many times do I have to ask you to take your pills?"	"Here are your pills and a glass of water."
"I don't have time for this (you) right now."	"If you could give me 20 minutes, I can pay attention to just you."

Week 5

Compromise

Introducing Compromise

Developing Cognitive Flexibility

Week 5

Parenting Skills Outline

Compromise

- Review the use of "new skills" at home, including **changes in verbal antecedents, list making, and changes in communication in front of children**. Validate and empower parents with troubleshooting.

- Discuss any changes in language that have helped them decrease the occurrence of non-compliance or verbal/ physical aggression.

  1. If you only have one person who recognized the changes, you are able to move along with the strength-based approach for the entire group.

  2. If your parents are having difficulty identifying change, use more examples from your own practice and experiences as a seed for recognition. Sometimes using personal examples from my own family allows parents to remember that we are equals attempting to work towards better solutions.

- Introduce **Compromise** (effective with all ages)

  1. The definition of compromise: *An agreement or settlement of a dispute that has been reached by each side making concessions.*

     a. Both sides have expectations.

     b. Both sides are willing to move toward the middle.

     c. Both sides are willing to give up on the less important components of the dispute.

     d. Both sides are winners in the end, because each person gains something from the interaction.

  2. **Compromise** is a tool that assists children with becoming more flexible thinkers, and better problem solvers.

     a. By teaching children to take the time to evaluate both sides of the dispute, you are able to slow down the internal system, which in turn decreases impulsivity.

     b. By teaching adults to take the time to evaluate both sides of the dispute, you are able to allow them to see opportunities for increased communication.

  3. If children and parents learn to be flexible thinkers together, then they have a tendency to learn to respond to changes in their world with less resistance.

     a. Avoid melting down every time someone makes a request or something new changes (i.e. substitute teachers, divorce/separation, or classroom changes).

  4. Compromise does not mean that you are "giving in." Compromise means that you are learning how to choose your battles more wisely, and invest your emotional time and energy in effective communication.

- Understanding **Compromise**:

    1. Help parents identify certain disputes that they are willing or unwilling to "give" on.

    2. Recognize that some things that they may be less willing to "give" on are often good examples of poorly invested emotional time and energy.

        a. Bedtime

        b. Eating

        c. Curfew

        d. Television/video game time

        e. Homework expectations

    3. Identify very specific disputes that they should never compromise on, which are usually legally regulated.

        a. Any safety issue, including which friends they are offered permission to spend time with

        b. Sexual behaviors

        c. Legal issues (including tobacco product use)

        d. Any aggressive behaviors

    4. Establish with parents and children that compromise means: "You get *some* of what you want, and your parents also get *some* of what they want, and you meet in the middle."

        a. This does not mean that one person gets **all** of their own demands, but that it is more of a balance scale of meeting in the middle on an agreement.

    5. Use examples of compromise.

    6. Help parents recognize that compromise actually allows them to save poorly invested emotional time and energy in the end, and helps prevent hours of argument and recovery.

- The **Steps to Compromise:**

    1. The child always **first** identifies what they want in the dispute or argument. If you allow children to say what they want after the parent has "put their deal on the table," then adolescents especially have a tendency to over balance the scale.

    2. Then the parent identifies what they want in the dispute or argument. Do not be afraid to let parents or children walk away from the compromise table to "think about their choice" more thoroughly before coming to discuss the dispute.

    3. Make sure that both parties understand that once they have brought their side of the dispute to the table, it is their final answer and they are not able to change their minds. Discuss and visually cue what "in the middle of those two wants" looks like.

        a. With young children I use a dry erase board to draw out amounts of food, or actually use a clock to show what time is being discussed. Remember that by pairing visual and verbal cues, you increase the brains ability to process in the cortex.

        b. I also try to help parents compromise in ranges of age, so that children do not have the same bedtime at 16 as they do at eight.

    4. Both parties verbalize (and visually cue) the final arrangement, which should be right in the middle of the demands. (i.e. The child wants to go to bed at 9:00 PM, but the parent wants them to go to bed at 8:00 PM. The middle is 8:30 PM, which we discuss verbally and pair with a visual cue on a clock).

5. Then we shake on it, which serves as a non-verbal contract and commitment to following through with their side of the agreement (resolved dispute). Do not allow either party to shake hands if they do not agree to follow through with the compromise.

6. It is that simply done!

- Discussion of the concept of **compromise** in advocacy within schools for adjusted workload with over-wrought students.

Week 5

Troubleshooting/Validation

It may feel like smooth sailing in your last few weeks of group, as parents become more invested in the techniques and offer troubleshooting and ideas to other parents more frequently in the first ten minutes. Be sure to revisit the basic building blocks of previous weeks each time you sit down at the table with parents. By doing this they are able to conceptualize their own novel approaches in their homes within those guidelines, and from a solid foundational skill set.

During this week of group, the concept of **compromise** is introduced and explained. It is vital to help parents understand that compromise is in no way giving in or being inconsistent as part of their new parenting approach. Compromise is a truly effective tool to aid in the development of flexible thinking and cooperative interactions within the household (and quite frankly, the school system too). I find this to be a most important parenting skill for families with severely behaviorally disordered children and youth, as these children often feel disempowered and disengaged from their world. Teaching compromise gives them an opportunity to feel like they have a role in communication rather than someone telling them what to do, or controlling them, all the time. When we give children with more severe behavioral problems a sense of responsibility, this allows them to become reinvested in the process of interactions with others. We see a decrease in co-morbid mental health issues, such as depression and anxiety, and we give children a sense of belongingness and presence in the family system.

During this week, I have a tendency to focus on emotional, as well as time, investments by parents. I often ask parents to think about how many minutes (or hours) they are spending arguing over nonessential disputes, such as bedtime, bath time, curfew, or how much food is eaten off their plates. This technique can be used for all ages, and aids in the establishment of healthy rapport within the family unit. In other words, by creating a family that talks more than it argues, those children and adolescents are more apt to access their parents without fearfulness or avoidance in the future. They are also more likely to be flexible and diplomatic in peer relationships and interactions with school professionals outside of the home.

After reviewing the time wasted with arguments, it is important to help parents identify where they are mis-investing time and energy that can be better spent enjoying their children (or doing things that are necessary for their own well-being, such as bathing and sleeping). When the group has two to three specific ideas to develop compromises around, discuss and practice the steps to effective and non-manipulated "middle ground." Be sure to help parents recognize that there are several areas that should *never* be compromised upon. Anything that can put their child in physical, emotional, or legal harm should never be up for discussion. Those are the times that it is important for parents to stick their feet and not "give in" (e.g. locally established and legally regulated curfews, drug or alcohol use, physical or verbal aggression, bullying/sexualized behaviors on social media, or promiscuity).

Emphasizing that both parties to the dispute must think very carefully about their wants and needs before coming to the table of compromise is an important first step in teaching the skill. I also think that when children see their parents thinking carefully about their side of compromise first, it teaches the child that this is a meaningful process that should not be taken lightly. I want parents to also allow children to think on their decisions before they come to the compromise table, as there are times that they didn't realize that the dispute was as meaningful to their parents as it is. I hear kids say, "I didn't know it bothered you that badly, and it's not that big of a deal to me, so I'll just do what you're saying."

The notion that the child makes their requests first as part of the balance scale is vital to this technique's success. Adolescents are likely to manipulate during this step, should the parents say what they want first in the dispute. For example, they may choose to stay out on the weekends until 6:00 AM as their side of the dispute. If adolescent identifies their desires first, the parent can balance the scales by saying, "Okay, then I want you home by 6:00 PM." If the parent goes first when bringing their side of the scale to the compromise table and says, "I want you home by 10:00 PM," then the middle ground would be 2:00 AM, which would not be appropriate for a 14 or 15-year-old.

Go through several examples of basic compromises (i.e. how many pieces of broccoli to eat, bedtime/curfew, how many towels must be folded in the laundry basket, etc.) to allow parents to understand that halfway does not mean giving only 20–30%, it means 50%. Be sure to teach parents to orally review the arrangement and incorporate visual cues to allow for neurological development for their child. In my practice, I use those verbal and visual cues to "make it stick," clarify any misunderstandings about each party's side to the dispute, and represent the process of "meeting in the middle" or "finding the middle ground." This is when visual cues come in handy for the processing component. We will also use the metaphor of balanced scales, to help both adults and children recognize that some weight must come from each to create a balanced middle.

Our brains have a tendency to encode and decode information best in sets of three, so by repeating the compromise three times there is more likelihood to recall and process this information internally. Assist parents in understanding that just because their child says what a compromise is in words, it does not necessarily mean that they comprehend or process that information accurately. They may ask that their younger children paraphrase for clarity, which is also teaching more active listening skills to our younger populations.

After the compromise is established, then it is time for the nonverbal contract. For many generations the handshake has been used as a symbol of trust and "keeping your word." Even very young children comprehend the importance of this gesture. That is why parent and child handshakes occur after a commitment to the compromise. This is in essence a behavioral contract, and does not necessitate a construction paper contract with signatures, stickers, or names written in blood. This is a good time to identify if someone refuses to shake hands, that they perhaps feel that they have not been met "fairly" on the dispute. The handshake is also a nice neutral reference point to go back to for the child, if they choose not to comply to the committed agreement later on. For example, I have many parents say, "Well, you shook on it, and that means that you need to be a person of your word." Often, the child will grudgingly comply while giving themselves an active opportunity to recognize how much less of a hassle it is to follow through with the commitment, rather than dealing with the consequences.

Now is a good time to reference the amount of time parents need to dedicate to the process of compromise. Usually, once the process has been established within the household it takes less than five minutes to come to a normal agreement. If the child is asleep by 9:30 PM rather than 3:00 AM, following the meltdown, this can help parents recognize that the compromise itself is a better investment of time spent interacting with their children than the argument was in the past. It may not be the 8:00 PM that they wanted, but a significant amount of anger and recovery time is saved in the process.

I sometimes find that parents are slower to identify an opportunity to manipulate the compromise at a later date than children and teens are. This means that you may have parents return to the table at a later time wanting to alter a compromise after they have already shaken hands and made a commitment to it. <u>Do not allow parents to abuse compromise!</u> I tell all of the parents that I work with, "Think long and hard before you decide what you want in the agreement, because once you shake hands you cannot take back your commitment." If you attempt to alter the commitment after you have said you will follow through, then you are teaching children to manipulate and take advantage of an agreement system. This is absolutely not something we want to teach children to take into their academic and occupational interactions in the future.

We will (if time allows) help parents in class recognize that this technique can be quite effective in interacting in their own marriages and relationships with others. We allow parents to discuss sticking points with interactions and attempt to consider a compromise that would make the investment of their emotional energy in that relationship result in a better outcome. When parents begin to learn to identify potential for compromises in their own adult relationships, they also become increasingly flexible thinkers in their daily living.

HOMEWORK: Compromise on at least one persistent issue at home.

Week #5

Handout for Parents

Steps to Compromise:

1. Your child *first* says what they want.

2. Then you say what you want.

3. Talk about the "middle ground."

4. Verbalize and use visual reference for the final agreement.

5. Shake hands as a *contract*.

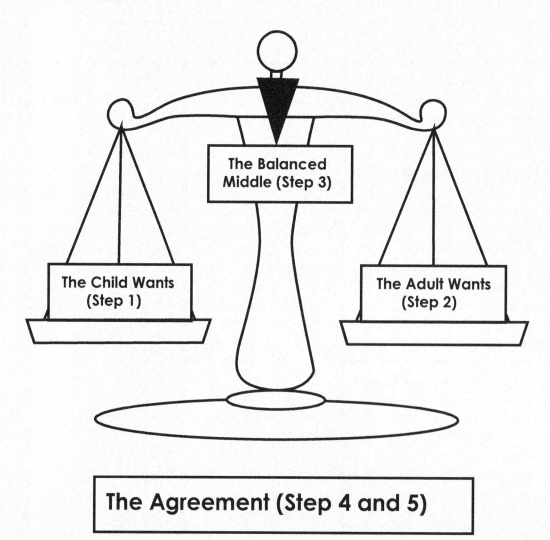

The Balanced Middle (Step 3)

The Child Wants (Step 1)

The Adult Wants (Step 2)

The Agreement (Step 4 and 5)

Week 5

Examples and Discussion Points

Example 1: Compromise

Johnny and his mom, Pauletta, argued over the drinking of a glass of milk for 11 hours. Why? Because mom was stuck in the "because I said so" mode and Johnny despised milk. This simple argument gained more power than it should have, and ultimately was fueled by negative emotion from both the child and the mom. How many of you have stayed up arguing until the wee hours of the morning about something (that just wasn't worth it) over of the premise?

Let's talk about "compromise." Compromise is when you get some of what you want, but not all of what you want, and you both meet in the middle on a dispute. Johnny understood halfway, but mom had a harder time with that because she was invested in "being a grown-up and being right." When it came down to the compromise, it turned out that mom was much more willing to "meet in the middle" when it meant that she could essentially gain back ten hours per night to do really normal parent kind of things, instead of using that time to argue over something as meaningless as a glass of milk. We had to determine the amount of milk that was being decided upon before coming to an agreement, which was identified as an eight ounce glass of milk not a 16 ounce plastic cup from a local convenience store. So, Johnny decided that from age 7 until age 8 he wanted to drink "zero glasses of milk (an empty glass of milk)." Mom decided that from age 7 until 8 eight she wanted him to drink "one glass of milk." Both of them got a little bit of what they wanted but not all of what they wanted, having a win-win situation, by meeting in the middle with half a glass of milk. We utilized a visual cue to help Johnny and his mother understand what a half a glass of milk was (use of a dry erase board and pictures drawn of empty, full, and half glasses of milk). Johnny and his mom committed, and shook hands on, meeting in the middle. Compliance occurred successfully for several months, because both parties in the dispute felt that they were being fairly represented.

Unfortunately, mom returned to the compromise table six months later and stated, "I changed my mind. Now I want him to drink two glasses of milk. I tried to get him to meet in the middle, but now he refuses." Upon review, Johnny was still seven. At that time, mom was told that she was not able to alter her side of the agreement because she too had shaken hands on it (made a commitment to following through with the compromise until he was eight). He knew that she was attempting to take advantage of him and abusing the system of compromise. Kids are really smart about something as cut and dried as compromise, and it's important to advocate for children when parents make an attempt to manipulate the middle ground.

Other examples of things that you might compromise on:

1. **The amount of food that is eaten at dinner.** Often times our portion sizes for children are more like adult portions which makes it difficult for kids to eat their meals in their entirety. Forcing children to eat all of what is served instead of eating until full also does not teach very healthy eating behaviors for kids. Utilizing compromise can give a sense of empowerment to children and allow them to have better self-awareness about eating behaviors and the sensation of "full." Also be aware, that some children are resistant to certain foods due to unidentified sensory sensitivities or food allergies. It is always important to discuss dietary needs with family practitioners and/or nutritionists to discuss the potential for these types of sensitivities, and alternative food choices to fulfill nutritional needs.

2. **Bedtime**. I hear from a lot of parents that want their children to go to bed by 9:00 PM, but spend most of their night arguing, crying, begging, and pleading with their kid until 2:00 AM or 3:00 AM. The argument that ensues regarding the perceived unfairness of that bedtime becomes the focus of attention in the family system, rather than the importance of sleep. If a child wants to go to bed at 10:00 PM, then the middle ground is 9:30 PM, which is saving several hours of argument and resolution while gaining sleep time for everyone.

3. **Homework**. I work closely with school systems in setting appropriate expectations for children and homework assignments. Some of the children that I work with have had upwards of five hours of homework assignments to complete each night. This type of expectation is overwhelming and seems "impossible" to some of the kids I meet with. I work with families to identify how long their children have been working before the quality of their schoolwork starts to crumble, and they begin to show signs of escalation. By identifying the length of time that they are able to commit to task-focus, we can communicate with schools on adjusted workload for home assignments. Those of you doing 504 or IEP planning know that we are able to adjust course load and classroom workload in much the same way. By teaching this as a technique of compromise, we are able to empower children to identify their limitations and communicate more flexibly with their world when experiencing frustration. We then see significant increase in the percentage of work completed following compromise, as well as the quality of production. In turn, this can assist in developing positive self-esteem and a sense of academic efficacy for even very young children.

4. **Telephone talk time**. In this age of technology, and 14 to 15 year olds (or younger) with their own cell phones, it is important to set limits about the amount of time spent talking on the telephone. In the past, we had basic rules for telephone contact. In the "good old days" it was considered rude and a poor boundary to call people's homes after 9:00 PM. In today's day and age, it is not unusual for children and adolescents to be calling or text messaging others into the early hours of the morning. Setting time limitations for the digital age can help teach common courtesy to children in regards to appropriate boundaries with peers and their family systems. Open discussion of a timeline, and compromise of the middle ground can be a helpful technique to teach children these skills.

5. **Video game play**. Many children do not have a significant amount of restriction on the amount of video game play they are allowed to participate in. The American Medical Association recommends that we have less than two hours of screen time in total each day, and that includes computers, video games, television, tablets, or other technology. I personally think this is an unrealistic restriction on our children, who spend much of their day at school utilizing instructional technology. I also think it is important that we have children that are not sitting for 10 hours a day on the weekend in front of role-play games and first-person shooters (to be discussed later). We also make attempts to wean children off of video game play, and compromise is an excellent opportunity to meet in the middle ground for the number of hours of exposure. It's important for parents to recognize that video game play is a key component of socialization for many of our young adolescent males. Therefore, you should recognize that limitations on time and exposure should match online gameplay, where the child has made a commitment to be a part of a skilled team. Downtime from the video games during these times especially should be avoided to decrease aggressive responses to these restrictions and "letting my team down."

Week 6

Being Aware and Involved

Importance of Peer Involvement

Increasing Parental Awareness

Use of Secret Code Word

Processing Exposure to Aggressive Technology

Week 6

Parenting Skills Outline

Being Aware and Involved

- Review the use of "new skills" at home, and review the **use of compromise**. Validate and empower parents with troubleshooting.

- **Introduce the importance of extra-curricular involvement**, which can assist with social skills training and managing impulse-control difficulties for both children and their parents.

1. Many parents express concerns about issues with transportation and financing involvement with extra-curricular activities. I make attempts to reframe outside involvement, not just as an opportunity for children to interact with others, but also as "a time of respite" for both parents and children.

   a. Several extracurricular groups offer tuition assistance, scholarship programs, and transportation assistance through youth service centers and YMCA programs. This can help children of lower SES populations to participate in these activities.

2. Be sure to have a list of available resources and activities that are appropriate for the child's developmental abilities, emotional control, and behavioral skills. Remember that extra-curricular activities are an opportunity for children to learn and practice skills that perhaps they are unable to do in homes or classroom settings.

   a. Helpful contacts:

      i. Schools (i.e. youth service centers or educational grant programs)

      ii. Community centers (i.e. YMCA or Salvation Army)

      iii. Social services (i.e. assistance through caseworkers, Guardian ad litem, or foster care provision programs)

      iv. Religious organizations (i.e. transportation programs for summer camps, etc.)

   b. Appropriate independent activities, especially for children who have had limited opportunity for social skills development in a same-age peer setting.

      i. Computer classes at school or the local university/community college

      ii. Girls/Boys Clubs

      iii. Big Brother/Big Sister relationships (can at times be accessed through case management)

      iv. Karate/Aikido (some parents are resistant to enrollment in martial arts, but these programs emphasize the importance of self-control before teaching other skills)

      v. Music (vocal or instrumental)

      vi. Afterschool programs for art, science, or cooking

    c. Excellent group activities:

        i. Soccer and tennis (limited physical contact sports)

        ii. Girl Scouts or Boy Scouts, or other organized programs with philanthropic outreach (also an opportunity to teach altruism and community involvement)

        iii. Art and science clubs

        iv. Religious youth programs or Sunday school programming (be sensitive to cultural and spiritual beliefs of parents)

- Emphasize the importance of parents being in attendance at anything associated with their child's extra-curricular involvement, to the best of their ability.

    1. It is important that parents who cannot be present due to health or work commitments, assist in finding at least one person who can be present to reinforce the importance of the child's participation/efforts.

- **Introduce Monitoring/Positive Communication/Protection Techniques:** (effective with all ages)

    1. Establishing an appropriate curfew (using compromise as necessary and as legally allowable).

    2. Creating check-in times for all ages of children to call home, or to their primary caregiver, and share plans or need for assistance with safety (much easier in today's society when children have access to cell phones). **Introduction of Secret Code Word.**

    3. Get to know your children's friends and the homes that they are visiting. Be sure to give examples of what might happen if parents do not familiarize themselves with their friends and friend's families: rape, abuse, neglect, illicit substance exposure, or kidnapping.

        a. Don't ever be afraid of appearing over-protective or annoying to your children, as it is your responsibility to ensure their safety even when you're not in their presence.

        b. Allow your children to recognize times when they feel they are unable to assert themselves appropriately with the negative peer population, and reach out for help to a primary caregiver.

        c. Establish an understanding that you are aware of your child's behaviors and actions even when they are not in your direct supervision.

            i. Do not be afraid to openly discuss appropriate and inappropriate sexualized behaviors and interactions with others (in public or in the social networking forum).

            ii. Research has shown us that by openly discussing avoidance of drug/alcohol use, we actually decrease children's likelihood of experimentation and overdose. (This is surprisingly important for children as young as nine to ten years old, as early childhood exposure to substances is on the rise.)

            iii. Help children understand that even if they feel pressured by peers, they have "an out" and that you are willing to "be the bad guy" in order for them to save face in interpersonal interactions.

    4. Establish regular meal times, as parents' work schedules allow.

        a. Even for parents that work second or third shift jobs, it is important to establish at least one meal a week when families are sitting at the table and interacting with one another.

        b. Remember the importance of removing any kind of technological distraction from face-to-face time with families.

        c. Avoid discussion of sensitive trigger topics at the table (those can wait for family meetings).

        d. Having regular meal routines increases appropriate communication in a family system and decreases eating related disorders.

5. Establish family meetings.

   a. Having regular weekly family meetings are an outlet for appropriate expression of frustration and problem-solution setting for parents as authority figures.

   b. Children are allowed to communicate their frustrations without consequence, as long as it is presented in a respectful fashion and with appropriate language.

   c. By allowing children an outlet of family meetings each week, you decrease the necessity for escalation, especially in interactions with siblings that in the past may go unnoticed by parents.

- **Introduce the effects of violent video game and television exposure** and how to decrease the negative impact on brain development.

   1. Identify how many hours each week children are spending in front of first person or role play video games that have violent context (not only video games, but also emotionally degrading television programming).

   2. Wean from violent media exposure.

   3. Change the impact of exposure through the options menus on video games.

   4. Teach processing violent media exposure to decrease the negative impact on brain development.

      i. Always process the perpetrator's perspective from a nonjudgmental stance (to develop cause-and-effect connections and create fantasy and reality separation with prefrontal cortex function).

      ii. Always process the victim's side (to develop internal limbic system response and emotional communication with prefrontal cortex processing to increase empathy and remorse).

Week 6

Troubleshooting/Validation

During this week, the discussion focuses on the importance for children to be exposed to same-age peers and peer interaction opportunities outside of the home. Finances, lack of transportation, limited resources, and limitations of free time for parents are the main reason they avoid extracurricular involvement for their children. While it is important that children have unscheduled/free-time, it is also important for them to develop healthy connections and social skills outside of the family and school contexts. Extracurricular involvement offers an opportunity for the development of self-worth, efficacy, positive self-esteem, and autonomy. I urge parents to access resources that perhaps they did not know were available to them in their communities. There are frequently assistance programs and scholarships available for low and middle class socioeconomic families (e.g. schools, social services, religious organizations, and within the extracurricular programs themselves).

Extracurricular involvement also does not necessarily mean it has to be a traditionally organized sports or other activity. Many of the children I work with that exhibit severe behavioral problems have "burned their bridges" in activities that require group involvement, focus, and team participation. Helping parents be creative about choices for extracurricular activities, allows them to understand that their child doesn't have to have on a uniform to be involved in an activity that is fulfilling to them.

Parents need to understand that one area of parental power in the home is that of showing appreciation and support for their child's efforts, even if they are not "very good at it." I have a lot of parents say to me, "No one tells me that they appreciate my hard work! Why should I tell them that they did a good job?" What better chance do parents have to parallel their own anger and feelings of disempowerment to their children's experiences, than recognizing that they wish that they felt appreciated for their efforts. These types of feelings can be caused by a lack of positive regard by family members. Often, parents find excuses to avoid attendance to school programs, sporting activities, recitals, etc. Parents tell me that they do not have time because of their work schedule and other responsibilities, and that attendance in these activities is low on the totem pole for prioritization. I ask parents to try to recognize that their appreciation for their children's efforts can have long-term impact on their ability to feel that they are participants in society in a positive way. I also recognize that it is difficult for parents to attend several activities each year, especially those that have more than one child in the home involved in an activity. This is an excellent opportunity to engage other family members in attendance, which assists in developing a more expansive support system for everyone. Having a healthy support system is vital to helping families' function effectively as "a team."

This is also the week that I urge parents to be more active in their knowledge of where their children are spending time, and with whom their children are spending time. Long gone are the days of being home before dark, or when the streetlights turned on. We live in communities that do not have that level of safety and opportunity for children to function away from direct supervision in a healthy or protected fashion. I also find that parents do not feel that they have the "right" to keep close tabs on their child's behaviors or peer interactions. We have some children and teenagers that wander the streets at all hours of the night, which is clearly a safety and protection issue. Curfew should be standard (with compromise as allowable), and phone calls should be made home if the child will be late (even if it's only five to ten minutes). Parents sometimes consider this a hassle or an infringement on their child's socialization, but it is important to remind them that in the world that we live in today the end result could be catastrophic. By giving attention to some of the impacts of limited supervision, we can help parents focus on keeping their children alive and well. If children are to be home after school with their guardian, then they should always check in before leaving the house to go somewhere else. If there is not a guardian in the home, discussion of negative issues with social services should be openly reviewed with all parents in the group. Many of the parents that I see who have been referred by social services, will share their own experiences with leaving children unattended "even for just a few minutes to run to the gas station." By allowing parents to share real-life references for the consequences of limited supervision, the group can develop a sense of empathy and increase personal self-awareness of their own responsibilities.

The parents in these groups also need to be taught to have a safety plan for missing children. The use of safe landmarks and passwords is quite appropriate for children from the ages of four to 18. For example, if a teenager is out with friends and uncomfortable with what their peers are preparing to do; we create a **secret code word** for them to use when checking in by telephone. If a child or adolescent checks in by telephone and uses the secret word, this immediately communicates to the parent that they are in an uncomfortable situation in which they do not feel that they can assert themselves away from a negative peer network. For example, if a child calls in and says, "My friends and I are going out to the park, and I was thinking about going and buying some 'bubble gum' before we went" (the word 'bubble gum' is the secret code word). This communicates to the parent that they need to come and get the child or adolescent immediately. This also gives parents an opportunity to say, "No, I think I want you to come home now" or "Do you need me to come and get you?" When an adolescent feels that they can lay the responsibility of disengaging from the peer activity on their parents, this actually creates a healthier belief that their parents are able to protect them while not losing face in front of their peers.

Even for young children, the use of secret code words is an excellent tool for identifying someone as "safe." I often have families that are unable to pick their children up from school or other activities, and send someone in their place use this word. This person can quickly identify to a small child that they are recognized as "safe" by the primary caregiver, simply by whispering the secret code word to them. Therefore, it is important to make this word secret from anyone other than the family members, and those responsible for transportation. Only share the word with trustworthy adults.

Reminding parents that communication is changing in the home will also assist them in being more proactive in getting to know their children's friends and families. Sitting as a family for a meal and helping the family prevent meltdowns with family meetings will also increase a child's belief that their parent is actually an "active grown-up" in their lives. I try to teach families that having regularly scheduled Family Meetings each week, even if only 10 to 15 minutes long, to voice frustrations within the home or with peers, can aid parents with personal self-awareness of negative peer interactions or potential for negative peer leadership. This can also assist parents in appropriately limiting their child's interactions with others, which can actually be a relief to an adolescent. If they can say to a friend, "No, my mom says I can't do things with you," it takes away the tension and embarrassment of saying, "No, you kind of make me uncomfortable and I don't feel like I want to hang out with you."

Family meetings should be regularly scheduled at least once a week, especially when trying new interventions or strategies in the home. This is a good time for parents to communicate the changes that they will be making, so that children can watch for them and give feedback as to whether they think they're "working or not working." I strongly recommend that meetings should be no longer than 20 minutes in duration, due to issues with concentration and task focus for all family members. The family meeting areas should be free from technology and outside distraction (i.e. cell phones, family pets, or visitors being scheduled during that time). The parent always starts and runs the meeting in order to establish appropriate limits between child/adult roles in the home. Teenagers often will attempt to use foul language and loud vocal tone during this time. While they should still be validated and their frustrations should be looked at carefully, it's important to identify healthier ways of communicating their frustrations. I ask parents to follow validation of frustration and paraphrasing with statements like, "Can you try to say the same thing now, but in a different tone?" or "I hear what you're saying, but I'm having a hard time getting past the cuss words. Could we try that one more time now that you know that I understand you?"

The goal of family meetings is not just simply to communicate frustrations, but to express concerns in an appropriate setting within the family system that is solution-focused. When families are able to communicate more effectively with their children during family meetings, they learn that they don't need to be upset about things that are really meaningless in the big picture. This is also a time to be solution-focused and openly discuss safety plans, or even role-play exactly what you should do when you feel uncomfortable in peer interactions outside of the home setting. It is important to help parents recognize that in order to "listen to your children" and their frustrations, you also must close your mouth and hear all of what they are saying. I find a lot of parents want to "run" the family meeting by constantly talking over their child or interrupting them while they communicate a frustration. For example, "Tyler is in my bedroom again and it's driving me—" gets interrupted with "We talked about Tyler being in your bedroom and then you went in his room too." This is doing the exact opposite of what you want to be, which is validating and discussing recurrent frustrations that perhaps have not been resolved with previous family meetings. Everyone gets an opportunity to speak during family meetings, and everyone needs to be heard and listened to.

In time, the relevance and severity of the topics during family meetings will decrease significantly. This is a positive sign that the family meeting activity is allowing parents and children to communicate more effectively on a daily basis, hence decreasing frustrations and unneeded meltdowns on a daily basis. Feel free to take a break from family meetings when the only thing you're talking about is "how bad mom's pasta is" or "how dad never puts the seat down to the toilet." Also teach parents not to be afraid to return to regularly scheduled family meetings if people begin to have difficulty dealing with old concerns in the home.

This is the week that we also discuss extensively the negative impact of violent video games and television programming on children. The first thing I talk about with parents is the amount of time that their children are spending in front of video games. This is a great time for us to become aware that the excessive exposure to first person aggressive video games or even emotionally aggressive television programming (i.e. any kind of program where people's emotions are being manipulated without having all the information, and a nation of people is watching to see how they respond— pseudo reality television programming) can be detrimental to brain development. By exposing our brains to this type of sensory information, without ever allowing for downtime or processing of the reality of consequences for those behaviors, we will continue to develop aggressive tendencies in our child populations.

First, we titrate exposure to aggressive media. If I have kids that are playing 10 to 12 hours of video games (in which they are shooting people's faces off, damaging property, starting fires, or stealing) the first thing that I want to do is decrease the intensity of that exposure. Parents often have a tendency to say, "Never mind, I'll just take that away from them." The sudden removal of that exposure can cause aggressive responses and escalation in and of itself. What we do instead is wean exposure in one-hour increments. So instead of sitting nonstop in front of a video game for ten hours, we will now play for one hour on and one hour off. What we will also do is enter into the options menu on first-person video games and change the perspective of gameplay from first-person to third person. By removing the component of "looking through the eyes of the killer" and changing it over to watching the behavior from a distance, we also decrease the negative impact of that exposure on the brain.

In the past, researchers thought that exposure to violent media material automatically created increased aggression or violence. What we know now is that even with violent exposure we are able to decrease the negative impact on the brain by taking the five minutes to process this information with our children immediately following contact.

There are two components to processing aggressive media exposure. The first of those is processing the perpetrator side. In order to develop healthy cause-and-effect connections and fantasy and reality separation for our child populations, we must take the two to three minutes to process the behaviors that are being acted out. So, if we are processing an aggressive video game, we will use nonjudgmental stance to question and say, "If you robbed someone's house in real life, what kinds of things might happen to you?" We make no judgment as to the cause-and-effect connection that children see, but allow them to internally reflect on what might happen to them "in the real world" if they perform these behaviors.

The second component is processing the victim side of the aggressive behavior. In doing this, we begin to tie the limbic system and prefrontal cortex function together, and create an emotive connection to behaviors. We are then developing skills of empathy and remorse. In order to process the victim side, we are simply putting children in the place of the person who is being aggressed upon and reflecting on how that might make us feel if it were to happen to us. For example, we might say, "If someone stole your most important things, how might that make you feel?" By simply taking the time to wean exposure, process the perpetrator side, and process the victim side, we decrease the negative impact of excessive aggressive exposure on brain development, problem solving, and emotive connection to our world.

HOMEWORK: Establish family meetings, create a Secret Code Word, and process at least one aggressive media activity.

Week #6

Handout for Parents

Communication Contract for Kids:

I know that going out with friends is a privilege that I have worked hard to earn, and I get to keep that privilege by following these steps:

1. When I am out with my friends, I agree to call home at _____PM and _____PM. If I do not call at these times, I expect my parents to look for me.

2. If my plans with my friends change in any way, I will call home and ASK permission before I do anything different than what we agreed on before I left the house.

3. I will let my parents know who I am with, and the contact information for the parents or supervisors that will be there. I know that my parents will meet my friend and their family before I am allowed to go without supervision.

4. I will follow curfew, unless I have obtained permission otherwise. I will call immediately if I know that I will not be home on time.

5. I will use the Secret Code Word at any time I do not feel safe, or I am uncomfortable with something my friends want me to do. My parents will help me *immediately* if I use the Secret Code Word.

_____   _____
Signature (child/teen)   Date

_____   _____
Signature (parent)   Date

Week #6

Handout for Parents

The Basics for Healthy Communication & Protection:

1. I need to have a regular curfew and check in time for all of my children, regardless of age.

2. I will be sure to know/meet every single one of my children's friends and meet their parents, before they are allowed to go and stay in another person's home.

3. I will schedule regular meal times in my house, so we have an opportunity to talk about friends and activities I may not have known about.

4. We will create a Secret Code Word for my children to communicate to me that they need help.

5. We will have regular family meetings, so that my children have a safe place to talk about their frustrations and I have a chance to help them feel less frustrated.

Week 6

Examples and Discussion Points

Example 1: What Could Happen If You Don't Know Their Friends?

I find parents to be quite resistant to the belief that a simple oversight on their part may have severe negative consequences for the lives of their children. I am never afraid to use the fear component to motivate parents to become more involved and aware of their children's interactions with others. I express to the parents that not every other parent is as concerned about your child's safety as you are, and making that assumption only sets your children up for dangerous situations (i.e. an unsupervised party at a friend's house).

A. Imagine that you sent your child to sleep over at a friend's house. You have never met that friend, or their parents, and you have no idea what their house rules are. You drop your child off at the end of the front sidewalk and watch them walk in to the front door, but never get out of the car to meet their parents or see what their friend's home looks like. Your child may not have a place to sleep that is appropriate, water to brush their teeth with, or heat. You would never know until a social services worker comes to your home to tell you that your child was removed because they were in a home that was neglectful.

Solution: Get out of the car, go inside of the house to meet their parents, and share your contact information. If it is not a clean home or appropriate for your child to be in, then take your child and leave. The anger that your child feels (and really embarrassment) is much less important than keeping them safe.

B. Imagine that you sent your 16-year-old daughter to a party at a friend's house. Because you didn't take the time to meet her parents, you didn't know that they think that it's okay for kids to drink alcohol, smoke marijuana, or have boys spend the night as long as it's in their home. You wake up to a phone call from the Emergency Room, because your daughter was beaten and raped by some drunk boys at the party and the parents didn't know upstairs, because the music was so loud.

Solution: Sign the contract with your teenager, and let them know that their safety is the *most* important thing. Openly discuss with your teenager how the use of drugs and alcohol can change the way you think about things, and put you at risk for being harmed or being taken advantage of by others. Make sure that your teenager knows that it's okay to call at any time they feel unsafe, and use their secret code word to ask for help. Again, know where they are and meet the people that are responsible for their safety while they are in that environment.

C. What if you sent your child to a friend's house after school? It was easy, they could just ride the school bus home with them after school with a quick note to the school. What you don't know is that those parents regularly use foul language in front of their children, have no curfew, and don't check to make sure where the kids have gone to. You get a phone call that your child was hit by a car on the main road, and no one knew where they were or how long you expected them to be gone.

Solution: Never allow your child to go to a home that you haven't visited first. Be sure that you have the contact information for parents and the child's friend before they go to the home. Kids still need to check in regardless of where they are, so that you know that they are in a safe environment. Better yet, schedule times for your kids and their friends to come to your home where you know they are all well-cared for.

These types of simple checks are for the protection of your children and to offer parents a sense a well-being and responsibility that they are still in charge even when not present directly with them. This seems like common sense, but I find that many parents are intimidated by their children and refuse to take precautionary measures because they "don't want them to feel uncomfortable." I also find the parents feel that they are too busy to take the time to follow these basic steps of security. How unfortunate would it be to lose your child over 15 minutes of effort not made?

Week 7

Keeping Up with Your Child's Changes

Behavioral Contracting

Journaling

Safe Word or Phrase

Week 7

Parenting Skills Outline

Keeping Up with Your Child's Changes

- Review the use of "new skills" at home, and review the **processing aggressive media, extracurricular activities, and getting to know your children's friends/family**. Validate and empower parents with troubleshooting.

- **Introduce Journaling:** (effective with all ages)
  1. Journaling does not have to be pages and pages of written information. In fact, the simpler the better (K.I.S.S.).
  2. Journaling should always review what the child has done correctly, even if only minimal progress has been achieved. This is an example of strength-based interaction, rather than loss-based interaction.
  3. Using examples of small progress monitoring and challenges to meet can be helpful for illustrating this tool to parents (e.g. "Today Robert had a hard time talking to more than one person, but tomorrow he plans to talk to Chris and his teacher.").
  4. Journaling should not be used as a negative record of a child's behavior, but as an opportunity to record what parents need to do to more effectively to support them in the process of positive change.
  5. Types of journals:
     a. Use of the standard notebook.
     b. Use of text messages tracking progress, giving reminders of goals/challenges, and offering support.
     c. Use of private messaging on Facebook or Twitter to follow progress with limits of "sharing" to private or family members only.
        i. If children are allowed to have social networking accounts, parents should always be on their "friends list" or "feed."

- **Introduce Behavioral Contracting:** (effective for all ages, but must be adjusted for age appropriate abilities and measurement. Be sure to use a visual aid!)
  1. Itemize goals and prioritize by difficulty.
  2. Identify the importance of daily review/consistent time and place for discussion of change and need for support.
     a. Do not process immediately before bedtime or dinner to decrease issues with sleeping and eating.
  3. Review the importance of "picking your battles," thus the contract is not to be used as a seed for argument or trigger for an emotive cycle.
  4. Each parent needs to create a contract for the child under supervision from the group leader to be sure that the contract does not become excessive or unmanageable.
     a. Remember the focus is on telling children what you *want* them to do, not what you don't want them to do.

77

5. Indicate that the best contract is one that is created with the child present to assist with empowerment and increasing attachment and connection within the parent/child relationship.

6. Practice and role-play daily review of goals, utilizing challenging language for children and thoughtful support.

- **Introduce "Safe Word/Phrase"** (effective for all ages and interactions with spouses and other adults in their lives, too).

   1. This is a technique to assist with establishing appropriate boundaries and recognizing when you have "hurt someone's feelings or body" enough that you need to take a moment to step back (consider it a tool to communicate to another person that they are "REALLY pushing your buttons").

   2. Define the safe word as "a humorous and rarely heard word, that immediately shuts down anger and helps children recognize that may have gone too far or caused them to cross over a boundary."

   3. Rules of **Safe Word** or **Phrase**:

      a. The family is to choose the word together.

         i. You can each put an idea for the word in a hat and choose from the collection of ideas.

         ii. You can decide as a family which word is the funniest, and therefore the easiest to identify or respond to in the heat of the moment.

         iii. You want to be sure that you do not use names of family members or pets in the home, because those are words you hear regularly.

      b. This word is to be used only when trying to communicate to another person that they have seriously stepped over a physical or emotional boundary.

      c. As soon as this word is used, it is a way to state to another person, "You need to take your hands off or stop what you're doing."

      d. If the word is being abused by any party, then a new word needs to be identified or chosen (remember that the learning curve tells us that after our first seven to ten days of utilizing a new word, there may be significant pushback and testing of limits, so don't give up after the first two weeks).

Week 7

Troubleshooting/Validation

This is essentially the last week of newly introduced parenting tools and techniques (although in the next week we will discuss developing an appropriate support system to help decrease dependency on professional involvement). Depending on the parents and their issues, you may include a discussion about different behavioral issues in regards to diagnoses. When discussing attachment issues and parenting skills, the focus should be more on the development of the relationship between the child and the attachment figure (i.e. parent or primary caregiver) more so than on compliance, to increase communication of needs. When working with autistic spectrum populations, recognition of sensory sensitivities and issues with transition, due to compliance with non-functioning routines and rituals, should be referenced as a hurdle in processing new parenting techniques. You may want to focus some of your group time on positive communication with social services and schools, or other information regarding medications and questions they may have about interacting with medical professionals. It really is dependent upon the character and members of the group. During this week, group tends to be rather self-run in regards to troubleshooting current issues in the home.

The three new tools taught this week for parents to learn and incorporate into their daily routine are **journaling**, **behavioral contracting**, and the use of a **safe word/phrase**. Journaling is especially important for foster families, those that have regular interactions with authorities/social services, and parents of attachment-issued children. Journals serve as a record of interventions being used as well as their child's response to those changes in the home. I recommend that parents take time at the end of each day to jot down progress in areas that could improve (or for which they could offer more effective support). The use of journaling also helps parents have a reference point to say to themselves, "Wow! Two months ago we had so many more problems than we do now, and look at all the plans we have to make it better." This experience in and of itself can be incredibly validating for parents who have experienced disempowerment and a lack of skills training in previous parenting classes or in interactions with support professionals.

Journals are an excellent tool for parental empowerment and do not require a significantly high level of reading or reading comprehension. They are for the parents to complete on their own. The use of pictures, simple words, and smiling/frowning faces can often communicate far more than several pages of specific notations. After a child and parent have begun to communicate more effectively, this technique can also be a family empowerment tool, which allows everyone to feel engaged during family meetings.

With higher functioning parents, who are able to verbalize and document change, I always recommend that journal entries be dated and have direct quotations from the child, parent, or other people involved with discipline or reinforcement contingencies. This is one method to resolve statements from children, such as, "I never said the 'F-word'" or "I don't remember telling you that 'I hate you'." By having the direct quote written down, you can reference the date and time of the interaction, and allow for accountability and responsibility for behaviors, without falling into "he said/she said" territory.

With my behaviorally-disordered youth families, I have a standard three–goal policy. No family should be working on more than three goals at a time to avoid issues with inconsistency and limited processing. (I also recommend this to residential facilities, foster homes, and school systems to assist with increased team consistency, as they do not need to think about 20 goals at a time and multiple agendas.) All parties should be focused on progress and strength-based momentum on a daily basis, rather than failures and developing negative self-esteem in our children. Journals can be an excellent form of recognizing goal completion, identifying goals that may require some tweaking, or areas that could benefit from more cognitive challenge by parents.

The format that I have found to be most effective and the least confusing for all populations, utilizes a small steno pad with four sections on each page. Points (i.e. measures of success, which can be changed into a percentage of success in comparison to the total percentage available for the week) are easily tallied by counting the faces and multiplying by the point value. This is not a token economy, this is a measure of percentage of change each week.

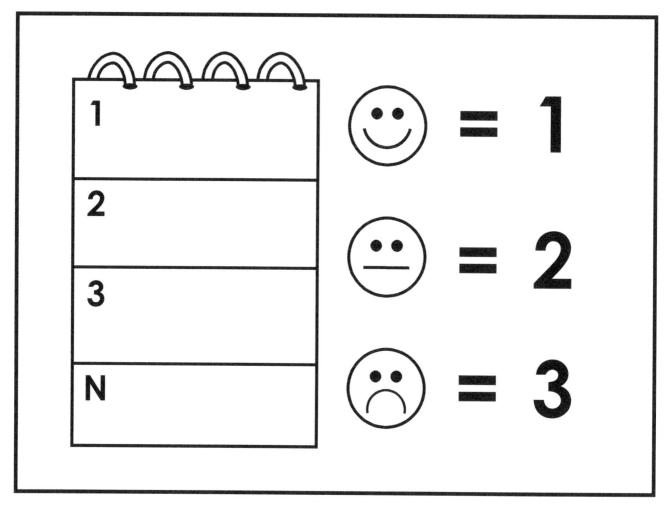

Sections 1, 2, and 3 are used to maintain focus on the three specific goals being set and working towards progress. The "N" section is used to help families make notes of positive changes in argument styles, exhibited effective communication, mature behaviors, and generally positive changes in their child's life. Not only is this beneficial for parents to refer to when they feel that "*everything* is falling apart," but this is also helpful for children to be able to recognize that their parents actually care about what's going on with them, and are involved and interested in their progress and successes.

Journaling can take less than ten seconds each day, and offers a great deal of information about the successes and failures of not only children, but team members as well. When we see consistent frowning faces in certain areas, this can be a signature that either this goal is too difficult for the child, or we as team members are not supporting effectively for progress. We are no longer going to work on the laundry lists of ineffective and unprocessed goals for six years, without making progress or tracking accountability. Now we are focusing on three specific goals to focus our energy on each day and the **journal** serves as a measure of change.

The second tool I like to introduce to parents is that of **behavioral contracts**. Behavioral contracts are not just a commitment between the child and adult to following through with goals, but also a tool to emphasize the importance of reviewing expectations together from a problem-solving stance each day. Unfortunately, many behavioral contracts have turned into point systems or token economies with many secondary gain-based reinforcements. Contracts do not have to be a stress-inducing argument between parents/staff and children and should be visual or verbal commitments to achieving goals on a daily basis together (i.e. completing chores, participating appropriately in family meetings, attending class, working well with same-age peers, interacting appropriately with siblings, etc.) Essentially, behavior contracts should identify the three areas needing improvement, and in each of those three areas, parents are to focus on challenging their child to move forward, rather than focusing on looking behind them (processing failures). This is strength-based model contracting, and helps develop positive skills for children like problem-solving, proactive choices, and accessing effective support for assistance when needed. By having a visual cue for success with goal setting, we also allow children to learn to have increased self-awareness of difficulties and needs to ask for help.

No one is expected to be perfect, least of all parents or staff who are overwhelmed. Children need an opportunity to recognize and change mistakes as they occur. If we do not take the opportunity to learn from our mistakes, and they continue unchecked, the persistent mistakes will fuel negative behaviors that are resistant to environmental interventions. Research has been clear about the positive impact of immediate feedback (the primary goal behind contracting) for developing healthier responses to similar environmental situations (generalizing). Being preventative, rather than responsive, can actually aid in increasing cognitive development, positive self-esteem, and healthy self-regulation.

I ask parents to identify three specific goals that they would like to work on each week within the home. Part of challenging language for goal development includes reviewing the mistakes that have been made in the past and what changes have been made in response. When identifying goals in any setting, it is important that one of the goals is achievable and well-practiced for the child in order to establish a sense of positive self-esteem and accomplishment. The second of those goals can be something that they are able to perform effectively about 30 to 50% of the time without significant assistance. The third goal can be something that is more difficult and requires more extensive assistive support from the environment.

Goal setting for our contracts can be relatively simple, and with those parents that have never set specific expectations for their children before it is important to start out with basic goals and work your way up. This is the time when it is important to revisit the notion of consistency, a foundational component of effective parenting. Inconsistency with goal review can actually impede progress and cause significant confusion for children. Many parents don't realize that by telling a child that they have achieved a goal, but then turning around and giving them 14 ways they could have performed better, sends mixed messages and creates negative self-esteem and self-worth. It is important at this point in group to review developmentally normal behaviors. This is the best way to have appropriate behavioral expectations for parents, as a 4-year-old cannot usually perform at the level that a 17-year-old can in some areas (although they may perform better in others). Help parents to recognize what is "normal" for certain age groups, and give them an opportunity to challenge changes in a positive direction as their children move through developmental milestones.

I help parents teach their children to brainstorm with several options for following through with the goal, and then to identify what consequences may occur from choosing those options. Remember, we have positive and negative consequences in our daily lives. I often reference this as "choosing your own adventure," which is about trial and error experiences in our environment and the consequences that can result from these interactions. By giving children options for following through with goals, we help them make increasingly advanced neurocognitive connections and increase their ability to process and follow through with expectations more effectively. Sometimes, we need to allow parents and children to explore poor decisions and behaviors to give them an opportunity to experience their mistakes. This is not dissimilar to having parents try to "live their children's lives for them." Sometimes the best learning comes from the experience itself, and allowing children and adults to have these experiences gives them an opportunity to gain self-awareness. Remember, it is okay for kids and adults to make mistakes; it is what you do with that knowledge that is the most important step towards progress. Think of all the mistakes you have made and how they have helped create a more well-rounded person from the process of learning (Example).

Goal #1

I WILL FINISH MY CHORES EACH DAY

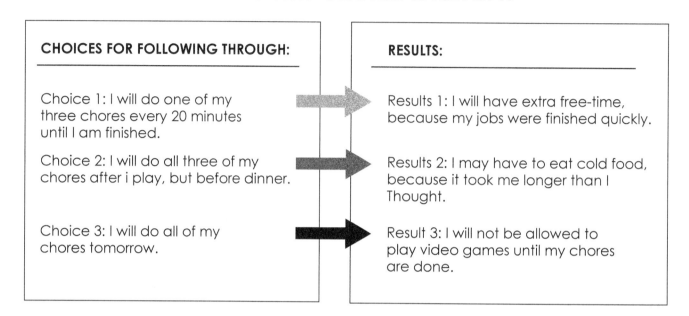

CHOICES FOR FOLLOWING THROUGH:

Choice 1: I will do one of my three chores every 20 minutes until I am finished.

Choice 2: I will do all three of my chores after i play, but before dinner.

Choice 3: I will do all of my chores tomorrow.

RESULTS:

Results 1: I will have extra free-time, because my jobs were finished quickly.

Results 2: I may have to eat cold food, because it took me longer than I Thought.

Result 3: I will not be allowed to play video games until my chores are done.

***We want to make the choice that gets us the best result and feeling (see handouts for parents to practice at home and staff to use at school).

The third tool taught in this week is **Safe Word/Phrase.** This technique is used to reestablish healthy boundaries, develop empathy, and create recognition in children that have difficulty understanding that they have "stepped over the line" with others. It used to be that safe words like "uncle" or "I give up" meant they were to stop our behavior right then because "you have hurt me in some way." In today's society, those words have lost their power and meaning due to excessive use and misuse, and therefore we must redefine boundaries through language in our homes (again, you can use a visual cue to assist with language/visual processing). This intervention can help families avoid three-hour arguments over remote controls or pain caused by excessive play fighting or wrestling that has "gone too far." Many of the children I work with state, "I didn't know I was bothering them," "We were all playing, but I'm the one that always gets in trouble," or "How am I supposed to know that I went too far?"

The rules of Safe Word/Phrase are quite simple, but following these rules can have a tremendous impact on healthy interactions in the home. By creating a new way of communicating, you can also create a new way of understanding your impact on others in the home and school system.

<u>Rules of Safe Word/Phrase:</u>

1. The word must be outside the context of normal conversation.
2. The word must be somewhat humorous
3. The word cannot be abused or loses its power.

This means that family names, pet names, words like "and" or "the," and any other word that is used regularly in the home should not be chosen. I have some families that have used "pineapple upside down cake" or "ladybug" to define their safety limits. The word should be humorous, because not only does that distract from the heat of the moment, but it also calms and soothes the amygdala and assists with internal self-regulation. In effect, the use of humor is a sly form of regulation that can pull people further away from the "fight or flight" response in their environment. Most importantly, if families use the word when not experiencing something significantly emotionally or physically harmful, then the word is losing its meaningfulness and power. This is almost a "crying wolf" use of the word, and decreases the efficacy of using the word for defining boundaries. That means that children (or adults) cannot use this safe word/phrase if they want to get their way, take toys or possessions from others, or manipulate for personal gain with parents (i.e. getting a cheese pizza from the grocery store or staying up later at night).

Parents and staff can be infamous for misusing this tool. Especially if a parent is tired or frustrated, the best option is to utilize the skill of parent's personal timeout to prevent saying or doing something that they do not mean, rather than using safe word/phrase to "get them out of my hair" for the time being. Children will also use safe word/phrase to their benefit in a negative fashion, if a parent teaches them and reinforces that it can give them a false sense of control over their environment.

It is not uncommon in the first seven to ten days of use of this word, to see "word abuse." Remember that in our first 14 days of any new technique we are simply learning how to adapt to the change in the environment, and we require 30 days before we can be sure if the technique is truly not working or if it's more of a measure of boundary testing. So how do we deal with that if we see "word abuse" occur?

What to Do If "Word Abuse" Occurs

1. In the first seven to ten days, we give a reminder of the power of the word to children.

   Example: "When you use that word to try to get the remote control from your brother, that is abusing the word. The remote control was not hurting your body or your feelings. I know you are probably feeling frustrated, but that's a good time to say 'I was watching that show, could you please give me the remote back?' We only use that word if something is really hurting our body or feelings, and that's what makes it powerful."

   ***Remember** to reinforce the appropriate use of the Safe Word/Phrase.

   Example: "When you and your brother started wrestling on the floor and your arm hurt because he turned it too hard, that was a good time to use (Safe Word/Phrase). That's the word that you use if someone has gone too far and has hurt our bodies or feelings. Great job using (Safe Word/Phrase) when you both needed it."

2. After the first seven to ten days (the time when testing limits starts to resolve), we can either identify a new word, following the components of an effective Safe Word/Phrase and state, "Now that you know how to use the word, and have had time to practice, let's come up with a new word that is our 'real safe word' for telling people they are hurting our body or our feelings."

3. After 30 days, if Safe Word/Phrase is still being abused (I find this happens more with adults than children), then perhaps this tool cannot be used in that environment until we have established improved communication.

It is possible for some homes to be incapable of using this technique, and that does not mean a complete failure of the system. It simply means that boundaries may be an area that requires more focus in treatment than other areas of communication in the family system. I find this to be especially true in households that have children with attachment issues, as these children tend to shatter and abuse boundaries more than other populations. Remember that children that have poor boundaries may also have parents with poor limits or inconsistency (i.e. their own attachment issues).

HOMEWORK: Start journaling behaviors, use behavioral contracts for goals and create a safe word/phrase for the family or classroom to utilize.

Week #7 (8 & Older)

Handout for Parents

Choose Your Own Adventure for Goals

```
                          ┌──────────┐
                          │   GOAL   │
                          └──────────┘
        ┌─────────────────────┼─────────────────────┐
┌──────────────┐      ┌──────────────┐      ┌──────────────┐
│  ADVENTURE   │      │  ADVENTURE   │      │  ADVENTURE   │
│      #1      │      │      #2      │      │      #3      │
└──────────────┘      └──────────────┘      └──────────────┘
```

What does this choice get you?	What does this choice get you?	What does this choice get you?
Feeling:	Feeling:	Feeling:
Consequence:	Consequence:	Consequence:
Do you choose this? YES NO	Do you choose this? YES NO	Do you choose this? YES NO

Week #7 (3-8 Years Old)

Handout for Parents

Choose Your Own Adventure

Draw the GOAL and your choices for getting there

1. What does it get you?
2. How does it make you feel?

Week 7

Examples and Discussion Points

Example 1: Goal Setting for Children

Remember that we want to have three goals for children to work on each week. One is relatively well-practiced and achievable, two is something that they are able to achieve most of the time but continue to require support, and three is something that may require new training or persistent support from their environment.

Goal Set 1: Help parents identify goals that are easily achievable or regularly practiced by their children. In this goal set, you may want to focus on chores that children regularly complete with little pressure or reinforcement from their environment (i.e. putting their clothes in the hamper, hanging their backpack by the front door, or putting milk back into the refrigerator). Although these may seem like things that should be on a chore list, they are also behaviors showing "respect for property" or "respect for others," and are actually behavioral goals that children are achieving at this time without recognition.

Goal Set 2: Help parents identify goals that require some regular reminders and redirection, but are achievable approximately 30 to 50% of the time without significant assistance or pushback. In this goal set, you may focus on communication skills in the environment, behaviors of sharing with siblings or same-age peers, or compliance requests for turning off technology (i.e. showing respect for their siblings by using verbal manners, passing serving dishes at the dinner table to others, or turning off the television set/computer/cell phone at bedtime).

Goal Set 3: Help parents identify goals that they wish to introduce or significantly improve upon, or perhaps goals they did not realize were important to practice for their child's success not only in the home environment. In this goal set, you may want to focus attention on self-regulation goals (i.e. calming down before "going off"), more extensive communication goals (i.e. asking for help when I'm frustrated), or social skills (i.e. using a coping skill instead of hitting peers on the school bus or at home).

Week 8

Graduation

The Final Session
An Effective Support Net

.

Week 8

Parenting Skills Outline

Graduation

- Review uses of "new skills" at home and troubleshoot with parents.

- Validate that some parents may be anxious about attempting skills at home without support from group.
    1. Discuss "boosters," which may be as simple as a quick phone call to the group leader with reminders about how to troubleshoot their current skills, or simply returning to review handouts or outlines from group.

- **Discuss the Importance of a Support Net**
    1. How do we choose appropriate people to effectively support us when we are not in treatment or support settings?
    2. How do we keep appropriate boundaries and not mistreat people in our support system?
    3. Why is having support (not just for children but for ourselves, as adults) important?

- Identify problem areas of parenting for each group of parents (allow the group to problem-solve together, to communicate added support, and validate those experiences).

- Quiz specific difficulties within that group.

- Praise and constructive criticism.

- Give Certificate of Completion and remind them that they have *earned* their graduation.

- Release.

Week 8

Troubleshooting/Validation
for Graduation

This is a week filled with praise and recognition for parents and their accomplishments. They deserve it! During this week, don't forget to troubleshoot the new skills used in the home. Parents may need some special time to resolve concerns about challenging language and contracting for goal achievement. Allow the rest of the group to brainstorm and role-play some of the more basic interactions.

During this week, I also help parents understand that they are capable of using these skills in their home long after they attend group. Many parents ask, "How long will I have to use these things with my children?" I usually tell them "forever." These are not tools just to be used while you're attending a group session, but changes for living that will help them for years to come as their children change and develop. The example I use is that of chronic dieters. Those people that gain and lose weight with diet and exercise, but have a tendency to return to their old habits and behaviors the moment that they lose the amount of weight that they want to. The problem with this mentality is that you constantly struggle with weight gain and loss, and never achieve stability. Stability for chronic dieters only happens when they change their lifestyle and make all of those good habits a part of their everyday living.

Positive parenting is a very similar concept. If you only use effective parenting skills when the going gets rough, then you're more likely to have to return to counseling or group treatment over and over again. If parents learn to incorporate these new skills into their everyday living, then their own behaviors become habit forming in a good way. By maintaining consistency all the time, not just when things are difficult, you teach your children that you are reliable, predictable, and trustworthy to them. This belief by our children can only foster healthy communication in the home, respectful treatment, and effective adult living. I tell all parents that come to group or family counseling that "this is a lifestyle change, not an antibiotic."

This is the time in group when I discuss the negative impact of having ineffective support systems. We have a tendency to turn to people that are available to us, but are not always effective in our daily living. Many of the families that I work with have a system of family dysfunction, which results in "drama" or other behaviors that undermine positive parenting success. Although you may want to turn to someone in your family, they may have been a thorn in your side or a negative role model for difficulties in the past. It is important to select people in our support system (what I call a support net) that are not just available, but also effective in helping us feel confident, maintain consistency, and that are supportive of our stability (even if the things we are doing with our children may be unfamiliar to them). I also teach parents that by having an effective support net and people to turn to in your environment it decreases dependency on the need for intervention either therapeutically, through the social services system, or in school.

Sometimes we need to be creative about who we choose to invite into our support net, and that means opening our eyes to opportunities for peer involvement outside of our comfort zone. I have some parents that eventually turn to staff members in the school as appropriate support net members, because those individuals have been constant cheerleaders and support any change within the family systems that affects children in a positive way. As we have removed the "them vs. us" mentality, some parents actually will turn to social workers and people in community settings to ask for support when they are feeling overwhelmed. Just as it is important to teach our children to ask for help when needed, it is important to recognize when we as adults need outside assistance. By having an effective support net, we have preemptively identified people who are approachable, willing, and supportive of our goals for success.

While the ultimate goal is for parents to be successful autonomously, if they have forgotten how to handle a certain situation or need a reminder of developmentally appropriate changes, they should be able to access you for boosters. I have a standard rule for "Parenting Boosters": If any one parent calls for boosters more than three times in one month then they may need to return for some brief one-on-one intervention or maybe return for another group. Parents that return for a second group have an opportunity to be validated in the changes that they had made when comparing themselves to new group participants. If they return to group for a second time, I try to give them an opportunity to teach other parents and support the notion that they have "come leaps and bounds in their understanding of the skills." By allowing parents to take on a teaching role in the group setting, or even asking them to join as a guest speaker, we allow them to build self-confidence and crystallize skills that in the past required a lot of energy to think about before doing. Parents that have a tendency to call more frequently, usually have their own issues with self-efficacy and self-confidence in the home. By having them return as a veteran to group, they can help develop positive self-esteem when they recognize that they are now the more knowledgeable person in the group setting.

Have questions prepared for group on this day that focus on the specific difficulties of that individual group. Maybe this group had a difficult time with the idea of flexible thinking, whereas other groups may have had trouble getting off the ground with differences between reinforcement and bribery. Focus "quiz questions" on those areas specifically, and give parents an opportunity to show their knowledge and shine. This is an incredibly validating experience for parents who have been disempowered by being involved in "the system" for several years.

Do not forget to hand out certificates of completion for all parents. This serves as a visual reminder that they were able to move forward in a process of learning, practice new skills, and become masters of their own domain. Some parents throw their certificates away, but others keep them as a reminder that they are capable of following through and changing their household structure. I also give out certificates to parents because it decreases the necessity for me to have to write letters to the court system or lawyers about attendance, participation, or completion. As always, be sure to have the appropriate releases for all members of the group.

Congratulations to you, too! You have successfully completed a rather intense eight-week parenting program and helped more than just those that are sitting in the room. By becoming teachers and equals, validating and sharing new information, and being flexible in our response to these group members, you have created an opportunity for these families to be successful, and made a positive impact on your entire community.

Week #8

Handout for Parents

Who is an Effective/Ineffective Support Net Member?

Ask yourself:

1. Who can I count on being there for me even when things are difficult?

2. Who feeds my anger when I sit down and talk to them?

3. Who seems to know how to calm me down the best?

4. Who seems to have good answers to my questions?

5. Who seems to care about me?

6. When are my most difficult times of the day or week?

7. Who has helped me in the past, even when family members were not there for me?

8. Who seems to understand my problems the best?

9. Who accepts me even when I'm at my lowest point?

10. Who seems to have my best interests, and my children's best interests, at heart?

Week #8

Handout for Parents

Invitations for My Support Net

I would like to ask you to be in my support network. Whether I'm having a really bad day and I need to talk about my feelings, or I'm having a really great day and I want to share my success with you; I would like to ask you to be there for me. I know that this is a big responsibility and commitment, and I want to respect our relationship. I only ask people that I trust completely, and that I feel are good people to help me be stronger.

So, I would like to ask you to be there for me M/T/W/Th/F/Sa/Su (circle the days) during these times _____AM to _____PM. I promise you that I will not ask you to do something for me that you have not made a commitment to. I also want you to know that I am trying to do my best on my own, and will only turn to you when I feel like I absolutely need help. Please let me know if you agree to be in my support net by calling or e-mailing your RSVP.

Thank you for considering being there for me.

_____
Signature

Parenting Clinic Diploma

This certificate recognizes that

_____
Name

successfully participated in and completed

____ / 8 Parent Skills Training classes

on this date: _____

_____
Signature of Trainer

_____
Date

References

AACAP (2002). Practice parameter for the prevention and management of aggressive behavior in child and adolescent psychiatric institutions, with special reference to seclusion and restraints. *Child and Adolescent Psychiatry*, 41 (2S), 4S-25S. Practice Parameter Statement by the American Academy of Child and Adolescent Psychiatry.

ABIDIN, R.R. (1983) *Parenting Stress Index—Manual.* Virginia: Pediatric Psychology Press.

ABIKOFF, H., HECHTMAN, L., & KLEIN, R. G., ET AL. (2004). Adding psychosocial therapy to methylphenidate may not improve its effectiveness in stimulant responsive children with ADHD. *Journal of the American Academy of Child & Adolescent Psychiatry*, 43, 802-811.

AFIFI, T. O., MOTA, N. P., DASIEWICZ, P., MACMILLAN, H. L., & SAREEN, J. (2012). Physical punishment and mental disorders: Results from a nationally representative US sample. *Pediatrics*, *130*(2), 184-192.

AGGLETON, JP (2000). *The amygdala: A functional analysis.* Oxford, UK: Oxford University Press.

ALEXANDER, J.F. & PARSONS, B.V. (1982) *Functional family therapy.* California: Brooks Cole.

AMATO, P.R. & KEITH, B. (1991) Parental divorce and the well-being of children: A meta-analysis. *Psychological Bulletin*, 110, 26-46.

American Psychiatric Association. (2013). *Diagnostic and statistical manual of mental disorders* (5th ed.). Arlington, VA: American Psychiatric Publishing.

AMEN, D.G. (2001). *Healing ADD: The breakthrough program that allows to see and heal the six types of ADD.* New York: G.P. Putnam's Sons.

AMINGER, G.P., PAPE, S., ROCK, D., ROBERTS, S., SQUIRES-WHEELER, E., KESTEMBAUM, C. & ERLENMEYER-KIMLING, L. (2000). The New York high-risk project: Comorbidity for Axis I disorders is preceded by childhood behavioral disturbance. *Journal of Nervous & Mental Disease*, 188 (11), 751-756.

AMINI, F, LANNON, R. & LEWIS, T. (2001). *A general theory of love.* New York: Vintage.

ANDERSON, C.A. & BUSHMAN, B.J. (2001). Effects of violent games on aggressive behavior, aggressive cognition, aggressive affect, physiological arousal, and prosocial behavior: A meta-analytic review of the scientific literature. *Psychological Science*, 12, 353-358.

ANDERSON, R. & PICHERT, J. (1978). Recall of previously unrecallable information following a shift in perspective. *Journal of Verbal Learning and Verbal Behavior*, 17 (1), 12.

ARON, A. R., SHOHAMY, D., CLARK, J., MYERS, C., GLUCK, M. A., & POLDRACK, R. A. (2004). Human midbrain sensitivity to cognitive feedback and uncertainty during classification learning. *Journal of neurophysiology*, *92*(2), 1144-1152.

ARTZ, S, NICHOLSON, D., HALSATT, E. & LARKE, S. (2001). *Guide for needs assessment for youth.* Victoria, B.C.: University of Victoria Child and Youth Care.

ARYA, S. (1989). In nutrition in mother-child dyad. *Indian Journal of Clinical Psychology*, 16, 34-40.

BALL, G. G. (1993). Modifying the behavior of the violent patients. *Psychiatric Quarterly* (historical archive), 64 (4), 359-369.

BATH, H. (1994). The physical restraint of children: Is it therapeutic? *American Journal of Orthopsychiatry*, 64 (1), 40-49.

BACK, A. (1999). *Prisoners of hate: the cognitive basis of anger, hostility, and violence.* New York: Harper Collins.

BALTODONO, H.M., MATHUR, S.R. & RUTHERFORD, R.B. (2005). Transition of Incarcerated Youth with Disabilities across Systems and into Adulthood. *Exceptionality*, 13 (2), 103-124.

BANDURA, A. (1984). Exercise of personal agency through the self-efficacy mechanism. In *Self-Efficacy: Thought Control of Action* (Eds.) R. Schwartzer. Washington, DC: Hemisphere Publishing Company.

BATH, H. (1994). The physical restraint of children: is it therapeutic? *American Journal of Orthopsychiatry*, 64 (1), 40-49.

BECKER-WEIDMAN, A. (2006). Treatment for children with trauma-attachment disorders: Dyadic developmental psychotherapy. *Child and Adolescent Social Work Journal*, *23*(2), 147-171.

BECKER-WEIDMAN, A., & HUGHES, D. (2008). Dyadic Developmental Psychotherapy: an evidence-based treatment for children with complex trauma and disorders of attachment. *Child & Family Social Work*, *13*(3), 329-337.

BEDELL, J.R. & ARCHER, R.P. (1980). Peer managed token economies: evaluation and description. *Journal of Clinical Psychology*, 36 (3), 716-722.

BELKE, E., MEYER, A.S. & DAMIAN, M.F. (2005). Refractory effects and picture naming as assessed in a semantic blocking paradigm. *The Quarterly Journal of Experimental Psychology: Section A*, 58 (4), 667-692.

BENARD, B. (2004). *Resiliency: What we have learned.* San Francisco: West Ed.

BENDER, E. (2004). PTSD, Other disorders evident in kids who witnessed domestic violence. *Psychiatric News*, 39 (11).

BERNE, E. (1961). *Transactional analysis in psychotherapy.* New York: Grove Press, Inc.

BERNSTEIN, N. (1996) *Treating the unmanageable adolescent: A guide to oppositional defiant and conduct disorders.* New Jersey: Aronson.

BEAUCHINE, T.P., KATKIN, E.S., STRESSBERG, Z. & SNARR, J. (2001). Disinhibitory psychopathology and male adolescents: Discriminating conduct disorder from attention-deficit/hyperactivity disorder through concurrent assessment of multiple autonomic states. *Journal of the American Academy of Child & Adolescent Psychiatry*, 40 (10), 1222-1230.

BLUESTONE, H. (2004). *Youth violence; prevention, intervention, and social policy.* Washington, DC: American Psychiatric Publishing.

BORNSTEIN, R. & PITTMAN, T. (1992). *Perception without awareness: Cognitive, clinical, and social perspectives.* New York: Guilford Press.

BOUDEWYN, A.C. & LEIM, J.H. (2004). Childhood sexual abuse as a precursor to depression and self-destructive behavior and adulthood. *Journal of Traumatic Stress*, 8 (3), 445-459.

BOULTON, M.J., TRUEMAN, M., CHAU, C., WHITEHEAD, C. & AMATAYA, K. (1999) Concurrent and longitudinal links between friendship and peer victimization: Implications for befriending interventions. *Journal of Adolescence*, 22, 461-466.

BRACKETT, M. A., & MAYER, J. D. (2003). Convergent, discriminant, and incremental validity of competing measures of emotional intelligence. *Personality and Social Psychology Bulletin*, *29*(9), 1147-1158.

BRADFIELD, R.H. (1970) *Behavior modification: The human effort.* San Francisco, CA: Dimensions Publishing Company.

BRADLEY, S. (2000). *Affect regulation and the development of psychopathology.* New York: Guilford Press.

BRENDTRO, L., NESS, A. & MITCHELL, M. (2001). *No disposable kids.* Longmont, CO: Sopris West.

BRENDTRO, L., BROKENLEG, M., & VAN BOCKERN, S. (2002). *Reclaiming youth at risk: Our hope for the future.* Bloomington, IN: National Educational Service.

BRENDTRO, L., BROKENLEG, M. & VAN BOCKERN, S. (2004). The resilience code. *Reclaiming Children and Youth*, 12 (4), 194-200.

BRENDTRO, L. &SHAHBAZIAN, M. (2004). *Troubled children and youth: Turning problems into opportunities.* Champaign, IL: Research Press.

BRONFENBRENNER, U. (1979). *The ecology of human development.* Cambridge: Harvard University Press.

BUNGE, S. A., DUDUKOVIC, N. M., THOMASON, M. E., VAIDYA, C. J., & GABRIELI, J. D. (2002). Immature frontal lobe contributions to cognitive control in children: evidence from fMRI. *Neuron*, *33*(2), 301-311.

BURKE, J. D., LOEBER, R., LAHEY, B.B. & RATHOUZ, P.J. (2005). Developmental transitions among affected and behavioral disorders and adolescent boys. *Journal of Child Psychology and Psychiatry*, 46 (11), 1200.

BUSCH, AB. & SHORE, M.F. (2000). Seclusion and restraint: A review of recent literature. *Harvard Review of Psychiatry*, 8 (5) 261-270.

BUSHMAN, B.J. & HEUSMANN, L.R. (2001). *Effects of televised violence on aggression.* In D. Singer & J. Singer (Eds.), Handbook of Children and the Media. Thousand Oaks, CA: Sage Publications.

BUSSING, R., ZIMA, B.T. & BELIN, T.R. (1988). Differential access to care for children with ADHD and special-education programs. *Psychiatric Services*, 49, 1226-1229.

CAMERON, J. & PIERCE W. D. (1994). "Reinforcement, reward, and intrinsic motivation: A meta-analysis." *Review of Educational Research* 64: 363–423.

CANFIELD, J., HANSEN, M.V., HANSEN, P., & DUNLAP, I. (1999). *Chicken soup for the preteen soul.* Deerfield Beach, FL: Health Communications, Inc.

CANFIELD, J., HANSEN, M.V., & KIRBERGER, K. (2000). *Chicken soup for the teenage soul III.* Deerfield Beach, FL: Health Communications, Inc.

CASHELL, M.L. (2002) Child and adolescent psychological assessment: Current clinical practices and the impact of managed-care. *Professional Psychology: Research and Practice*, 33 (5), 446-453.

CASTLE, S.E. (1996). *Personal Communication.*

CHAMBERLAIN, P. (2003). *Treating chronic juvenile offenders: Advances made through the Oregon multidimensional treatment foster care model.* Washington, DC: an American Psychological Association.

CHARD, K.M., WEAVER, T.L. & RESICK, P.A. (1997). Adapting cognitive processing therapy for child sexual abuse survivors. *Cognitive and Behavioral Practice*, 4, 31-52

CLARK, L. (1996). *S.O.S. for parenting: A practical guide for handling everyday behavior problems* (Second Edition). Bowling Green, KY: Parents Press.

CLARK, L. (1998). *S.O.S. help for emotions: Managing anxiety, anger, and depression.* Bowling Green, KY: Parents Press.

CRICK, N.R. & DODGE, K.A. (1996) Social information processing mechanisms in reactive and proactive aggression. *Child Development*, 67, 993-1002.

COLE, P.M., ZAHN-WAXLER, C., FOX, N.A., USHER, B.A. & WELSH, J.D. (1996). Individual differences and emotion regulation and behavior problems and preschool children. *Journal of Abnormal Psychology*, 105 (4), 518-529.

CONDUCT PROBLEMS PREVENTION RESEARCH PROGRAM. (1992) A developmental and clinical model for the prevention of conduct disorder. *Developmental Psychopathology*, 4, 509-527.

CONNOR, D.F. (2002). Preschool Attention Deficit Hyperactivity Disorder: A review of prevalence, diagnosis, neurobiology, and stimulant treatment. *Journal of Developmental & Behavioral Pediatrics*, 23 (0), S1-S9.

CORRIGAN, P.W. (1991). Strategies that overcome barriers to token economies in community programs for severe mentally ill youth. *Community Mental Health Journal*, 27 (1), 17-30.

COSTELLO, E. J., MUSTILLO, S., ERKANLI, A, KEELER, G. & ANGOLED, A. (2003). Prevalence and development of psychiatric disorders in childhood and adolescence. *Archived General Psychiatry*, 60, 837-844.

COTTON, N.U., RESNICK, D.C., BROWNE, S.L., MARTIN, D. R., MCCARRAHER, J. & WOODS, J. (1994). Aggression and fighting behavior among African-American adolescents: Individual and family factors. *American Journal of Public Health*, 84, 618-622.

CURRIE, J. & THOMAS, D. (1995). Does head start make a difference? *American Economic Review*, 85 (3), 341-364.

DARLING, N., & STEINBERG, L. (1993). Parenting style as context: An integrative model. *Psychological bulletin*, *113*(3), 487-496.

DAY, D. M. (2002). Examination therapeutic utility of restraints and seclusion with children and youth: The role of fear he and research and practice. *American Journal of Orthopsychiatry*, 72 (2), 266-278.

DAY, A. L., & CARROLL, S. A. (2004). Using an ability-based measure of emotional intelligence to predict individual performance, group performance, and group citizenship behaviours. *Personality and Individual Differences*, *36*(6), 1443-1458.

DECI, E.L., KOESTNER, R. & RYAN, R.M. (2001). "Extrinsic rewards and intrinsic motivation in education: Reconsidered once again." *Review of Educational Research* 71.1: 1–27.

DIGIACOMO, J.N. & ROSEN, H. (1978). The role of physical restraint in the treatment of psychiatric illness. *Journal of Clinical Psychiatry*, 39 (3), 228-232.

DISHION, T.J., NELSON, S.E. & YASUI, M. (2005). Predicting early adolescence gang involvement from middle school adaptation. *Journal of Clinical Child & Adolescent Psychology*, 34 (1), 62-73.

DOOLEY, P., WILCZENSKI, F. L., & TOREM, C. (2001). Using an activity schedule to smooth school transitions. *Journal of Positive Behavior Interventions, 3*(1), 57-61.

DOSREIS, S., ZITO, J.M., SAFER, D.J., GARDNER, J.F. & PUCCIA, K.B. (2005). Multiple psychotropic medication use for youths: A 2-state comparison. *Journal of Child and Adolescent Psychopharmacology*, 15 (1), 68-77.

DODGE, K. & SOMBERG, D. (1987). Hostile attribution biases among aggressive boys are exacerbated under conditions of threat to the self. *Child Development*, 58, 213-234.

DRISKO, J.W. (1981). Therapeutic use of physical restraint. *Child and Youth Care Forum*, 10 (4), 318-328.

DUMAS, J.E. (1989) Treating antisocial behavior in children: Child and family approaches. *Clinical Psychology Review*, 9, 197-222.

DURLAK, J. A., & WELLS, A. M. (1997). Primary prevention mental health programs for children and adolescents: A meta-analytic review. *American journal of community psychology*, *25*(2), 115-152.

EISENBERGER, R., PIERCE, W. D., & CAMERON, J. (1999). Effects of reward on intrinsic motivation—Negative, neutral, and positive: Comment on Deci, Koestner, and Ryan (1999).

EITAM, B, HASSIN, R.R. & YAACOV, S. (2008). "Nonconscious goal pursuit in novel environments: The case of implicit learning." *Psychological Science* 19.3: 261–267.

ENGLE, P.L. & RICCIUTI, H. (1996). Psycho-social aspects of care and nutrition. *Food and Nutrition Bulletin Supplement*, 14 (3), 201-220.

ERON, L. & HUESMAN, L.R. (1986). *Television and the aggressive child: A cross-national comparison.* Hillsdale, NJ: Earlbaum Associates.

FIORI, M. (2009). A new look at emotional intelligence: A dual-process framework. *Personality and Social Psychology Review, 13*(1), 21-44.

FIORI, M., & ANTONAKIS, J. (2011). The ability model of emotional intelligence: Searching for valid measures. *Personality and Individual Differences, 50*(3), 329-334.

FOERDE, K., RACE, E., VERFAELLIE, M., & SHOHAMY, D. (2013). A role for the medial temporal lobe in feedback-driven learning: Evidence from amnesia. *The Journal of Neuroscience, 33*(13), 5698-5704.

FOSHA, D., SIEGEL, D. J., & SOLOMAN, M. (Eds.). (2011). *The healing power of emotion: Affective neuroscience, development & clinical practice (Norton Series on Interpersonal Neurobiology).* WW Norton & Company.

FRICK, P.J., LAHEY, B.B., LOEBER, R., STOUTHAMER-LOEBER, M., M.A.G. & HANSON, K. (1992) Familial risk factors to oppositional defiant disorder and conduct disorder: Parental psychopathology and maternal parenting. *Journal of Consulting and Clinical Psychology*, 60, 49-55.

FRICK, P.J. Family dysfunction and the disruptive behavior disorders: A review of recent empirical findings. In: OLLENDICK, T.H. & PRINZ, R.J., editors. Advances in Child Clinical Psychology. (1994) New York: Plenum: pp203-222.

FRICK, P.J. (2000). A comprehensive and individualized treatment approach for children and adolescents with conduct disorders. *Cognitive and Behavioral Practice*, 7, 30-37.

FRICK, P. (2001) Effective interventions for children and adolescents with conduct disorder. *Canadian Journal of Psychiatry*, 46.

FRIEDMAN, S. (1994) *Staying simple, staying focused: Time-effective consultations with children and families.* In: HOYT, M. (Ed.) Constructive Therapies (pp 217-250). New York: Guilford.

GALLER, J.R. & RAMSEY, F. (1985). The influence of early malnutrition on subsequent behavioral development: VI the role of the microenvironment of the household. *Nutrition and Behavior*, a 2, 161-173.

GARDENER, W., KELLEHER, K. & PAJER, K. (2002). Multidimensional adaptive testing for mental health problems in primary care. *Medical Care*, 40 (9), 812-823.

GENDREAU, P., LITTLE, T., & GROGGIN, c. (1996). A meta-analysis of the predictors of adult offender recidivism: What works! *Criminology*, 34, 575-607.

GENDREAU, P. & ROSS, R.R. (1987). Revivification of rehabilitation: Evidence from the 1980's. *Justice Quarterly*, 4, 349-407.

GERSHOFF, E. T. (2013). Spanking and child development: We know enough now to stop hitting our children. *Child development perspectives*, 7(3), 133-137.

GIBBS, J. (2003). Equipping youth with mature moral judgment. *Reclaiming Children and Youth*, 12 (3), 149-154.

GIFFORD-SMITH, M., DODGE, K.A., DISHION, T.J. & MCCORD, J. (2005). Peer influence in children and adolescents: Crossing the bridge from developmental to intervention science. *Journal of Abnormal Child Psychology*, 33 (3), 255-265.

GILLET, N., VALLERAND, R.J. & LAFRENIERE, M.K. (2012). "Intrinsic and extrinsic school motivation as a function of age: The mediating role of autonomy support." *Social Psychology in Education*: 77–95.

GLENN, M. (2002). A differential diagnostic approach to the pharmacological treatment of cognitive, behavioral, and affective disorders after traumatic brain injury. *Journal of Head Trauma Rehabilitation*, 17 (4), 273-283.

GOLD, M. (1995) Charting a course: Promise and prospects for alternative schools. *Journal of Emotional and Behavioral Problems*, 3 (4), 8-11.

GOLD, M., & OSGOOD, D.W. (1992). *Personality and peer influence in juvenile corrections.* Westport, CT: Greenwood Press.

GOLDMAN-RAKIC, P. S. (1995). Architecture of the prefrontal cortex and the central executive. *Annals of the New York Academy of Sciences*, 769(1), 71-84.

GOLDMAN-RAKIC, P. S., COOLS, A. R., & SRIVASTAVE, K. (1996). The prefrontal landscape: Implications of functional architecture for understanding human mentation and the central executive [and Discussion]. *Philosophical Transactions of the Royal Society of London. Series B: Biological Sciences*, 351(1346), 1445-1453.

GOLDSTEIN, A.P. (1999). *Low level of aggression: First steps on the ladder to violence.* Champaign, IL. Research Press.

GOLDSTON, D. B., DANIEL, S. S., & ARNOLD, E. M. (2006). Suicidal and non-suicidal self-harm behaviors. *Behavioral and emotional disorders in adolescents: Nature, assessment, and treatment*, 343-380.

GOWDY, V.B. (1996). Historical Perspective. In D. L. McKenzie & E.E. Hebert (Eds.), *Correctional boot camps: A tough intermediate sanction.* Washington, DC: National Institute of Justice.

GREENBURG, M. T., DOMITROVICH, C., & BUMBARGER, B. (1999). Preventing mental disorders in school-age children: A review of the effectiveness of prevention programs. *Prevention Research Center for the Promotion of Human Development, College of Health and Human Development, Pennsylvania State University.*

GREENE, R.W. (2001) *The explosive child: A new approach for understanding and helping easily frustrated, "chronically inflexible" children* (2nd ed.) New York: Harper Collins.

GREENFIELD, P.M. (1984). *Mind and media: the effects of television, computers and video games.* London: Fontana.

GROVES, D., ZUCKERMAN, D., MARANS, S. & COHEN, D. (1993). Silent victims: Children who witness violence. *Journal of the American Medical Association,* 269, 262-264.

GUERRA, N.G., HUESMAN, L.R. & SPINDLER, A.J. (2003). Community violence exposure, social cognition, and aggression among urban elementary-schoolchildren. *Child Development,* 74 (5), 1507-1522.

HAGEDORN, J.M. (1995) *Forsaking our children: Bureaucracy and reform in the child welfare system.* Chicago: Lakeview Press.

HAGGER, M.S. & CHATZISARANTIS, N.L.D. (2011). "Causality orientations moderate the undermining effect of rewards on intrinsic motivation." *Journal of Experimental Social Psychology:* 485–489.

HAYAMIZU, T. (1997). "Between intrinisic and extrinsic motivation: Examination of reasons for academic study based on theory of internalization." *Japanese Psychological Research* (1997):98–108.

HAYES, S. C., MASUDA, A., BISSETT, R., LUOMA, J., & GUERRERO, L. F. (2005). DBT, FAP, and ACT: How empirically oriented are the new behavior therapy technologies?. *Behavior Therapy,* 35(1), 35-54.

HAYES, M. J. & REILLY, G. O. (2013). Psychiatric disorder, IQ, and emotional intelligence among adolescent detainees: A comparative study. *Legal and Criminological Psychology,* 18(1), 30-47.

HEALY, J. (1984). *Endangered minds: Why our children don't think.* Simon & Shuster, New York.

HERPERTZ, S.C, MUELLER, B., WENNING, B., QUNAIBI, M., LICHTERFIELD, C. & HERPERTZ-DAHLMAN, B. (2003). Autonomic responses and boys with externalizing disorders. *Journal of Neural Transmission,* 110 (10), 1181-1195.

HO, P.T., KELLER, J.L., BERG, A.L., CARGAN, A.L. & HADDAD, J. (1999). Pervasive developmental delay in children presenting as possible hearing loss. *Laryngoscope,* 109 (1), 129-135.

HOWES, C., JAMES, J. & RITCHIE, S. (2003). Pathways to effective teaching. *Early Childhood Research Quarterly,* 18 (1).

HUDLEY, C. & FRIDAY, J. (1996) Attribution bias and reactive aggression. *American Journal of Preventative Medicine,* 12, 75-81.

HUESMANN, L.R. & ERON, L.D. (1983). Factors influencing the effects of television on children: Learning from television: Psychological and educational research. Academic Press.

HUESMANN, L.R., ANDERSON, C.A., BERKOWITZ, et al. (2001). *Media violence and the youth violence (summary).* In D. Elliot (ed.) Youth violence: A report of the Surgeon General. Washington, DC: US Government Printing Office.

HUESMANN, L.R. & SKORIC, M. (2003). *Regulating media violence: Why, how, and by whom?* In B. Young & E. Palmer (Ed.) Children and the Faces of Televisual Media: Teaching, Violence, Selling. Mahwah, NJ: Lawrence Erlbaum.

HUGHES, D. A. (2007). *Attachment-focused family therapy.* WW Norton & Company.

HUNT, D.E. (1987). *Beginning with ourselves: In practice, theory, and human affairs.* Cambridge, MA: Brookline Books.

HOBBS, N. (1975) *The Futures of Children*. San Francisco, CA: Jossey-Bass Limited.

HYMAN, I., & SNUCK, P.A. (2001). Dangerous schools, alienated students. *Reclaiming children and youth*, 10 (3), 133-136.

JEFFREY, K. (2002). Therapeutic restraint of children: It must always be justified. *Pediatric Nursing*, 14 (9), 20-22.

JELLIFFE, D.B. (1965). Affected malnutrition on behavioral and social development. In *Proceedings of the Western Hemisphere Nutrition Congress*. Chicago, IL: American Medical Association.

JENSEN, PS, BHATARA, V.S., VITIELLO, B., HOAGWOOD, K., FEIL, M. & BURKE, L. (1999). Psychoactive medication prescribing practices for US children: Gaps between research and clinical practice. *Journal of the American Academy of Child & Adolescent Psychiatry*, 38 (5), 557-565.

Joint Commission Resources. (2000). *Restraint in behavioral health care: Minimizing use, improving outcomes.* (Videotape). JCR Tape Library. Oakbrook Terrace, IL: Joint Commission Resources, Inc.

JONES, R., & TIMBERS, G. (2002). And analysis of the restraint event and its behavioral effects on clients and staff. *Reclaiming Children and Youth*, 11 (1), 37-41.

JOSEPH, D. L., & NEWMAN, D. A. (2010). Emotional intelligence: An integrative meta-analysis and cascading model. *Journal of Applied Psychology*, *95*(1), 54.

JOURNAL OF SAFE MANAGEMENT. (2000). Protecting kids in restraint. *Reclaiming Children and Youth*, 10 (3), 162-163.

KANE, M. J., & ENGLE, R. W. (2002). The role of prefrontal cortex in working-memory capacity, executive attention, and general fluid intelligence: An individual-differences perspective. *Psychonomic bulletin & review*, *9*(4), 637-671.

KAPLAN, E. L. & MAYER, P. (1958). Nonparametric estimation from incomplete observations. *Journal of American Statistics*, 53:457-481.

KASTNER, J.W. (1998). Clinical change in adolescent aggressive behavior: A group therapy approach. *Journal of Child and Adolescent Group Therapy*, 8 (1), 23-33.

KAZDIN, A.E. (1987) *Problem-solving and parent management in treating aggressive antisocial behavior.* In E.D. Hobbs &P.S. Jensen (Eds.) Psychological treatments for child and adolescent disorder: Empirically based strategies for clinical practice (pp. 377-408). Washington, DC: American Psychological Association.

KESSLER, RC, MERIKANGAS KR, BERGLUND, P., DEMLER, O., JIN, R. & WALTERS, E. E. (2004). Lifetime prevalence and age-of-onset distributions of DSM-IV disorders and the national comorbidity survey replication. *International Journal of Psychiatric Methods Research*, 13, 60-68.

KING, J., & JUST, M. A. (1991). Individual differences in syntactic processing: The role of working memory. *Journal of memory and language*, *30*(5), 580-602.

KLEIN, S.B. (1987) *Learning: Principles and applications*. New York: McGraw-Hill, Inc.

KOERNER, K. (2013). What must you know and do to get good outcomes with DBT? *Behavior Therapy*.

KOOP, E. & LEEPER, B. (1992). Violence: A national emergency. *American Journal of Public Health*.

KRUESI, M.J., HIBBS, E.D., ZAHN, T.P., KEYSOR, C.S., HAMBURGER, S.D., BARTKO, J.J. & RAPOPORT, J.L. (1993). A 2-year prospective follow-up study of children and adolescents with disruptive behavior disorders. Prediction by cerebrospinal fluid 5-hydroxyindoleacetic acid, homovanillic acid, and autonomic measures? *Child Psychiatry*, 30 (6), 605-614.

LAHEY, APPLEGATE, B., BERKELEY, R. A., GARFINKEL, B., MCBURNETT, K., KERDYK, L., GREENHILL, L., HYND, G. W., FRICK, P.J., & NEWCORN, J. (1994). DSM-IV field trials for oppositional defiant disorder and conduct disorder in children and adolescents. *American Journal of Psychiatry*, 151, 1163-1171.

LARSEN, E. (2003). Frontiers in strength-based treatment. *Reclaiming Children and Youth*, 12 (1), 12-17.

LARSON, S. & BRENDTRO, L. (2000) *Reclaiming our prodigal sons and daughters: A practical approach for connecting with youth in conflict.* Bloomington, IN: National Education Service.

LEE, C.C. (1995) *Counseling for diversity: A guide for school counselors and related professionals.* Massachusetts: Allyn and Bacon.

LEPPER, M.R., GREENE, D. & NISBETT, R.E. (1973). "Undermining children's intrinsic interest with external reward: A test of the "undermining" hypothesis." *Journal of Personality and Social Psychology*: 129–147.

LEVY, F., HAY, D. A., BENNETT, K. S. & MCSTEPHEN, M.B. (2005). Gender differences in ADHD subtype comorbidity. *Journal of the American Academy of Child & Adolescent Psychiatry*, 44 (4), 368-376.

LEWIS, M. V. (2000). Reformulated attention-deficit hyperactivity disorder according to signal detection theory. *Journal of the American Academy of Child Psychiatry*, 39 (9), 1144-1151.

LICKONA, T. (2012). *Raising good children: From birth through the teenage years.* Random House Digital, Inc..

LITTLE, P.F.B. (2004). Peer coaching as a support to collaborative teaching. *Mentoring and Tutoring*, 13 (1), 83-94.

LINEHAN, M.M. (1994). The empirical basis of dialectical behavior therapy: Development of new treatments versus evaluation of existing treatments. *The Journal of Mind and Behavior*, 15 (4), 323-342.

LINEHAN, M. M., DIMEFF, L. A., REYNOLDS, S. K., COMTOIS, K. A., WELCH, S. S., HEAGERTY, P., & KIVLAHAN, D. R. (2002). Dialectical behavior therapy versus comprehensive validation therapy plus 12-step for the treatment of opioid dependent women meeting criteria for borderline personality disorder. *Drug and alcohol dependence*, *67*(1), 13-26.

LIPSEY, M. W., & WILSON, DB (1998). Effective intervention for serious juvenile offenders: A synthesis of research. In R. Lobar & D. Farington (Eds.) *Serious and violent juvenile offenders: Risk factors and successful interventions* (313-345). Thousand Oaks: Sage.

LOEBER, R., BURKE, J.D., LAHEY, B.B., WINTERS, A. &ZERA, M. (2000). Oppositional defiant and conduct disorder: A review of the past 10 years, part I. *Journal of the American Academy of Child and Adolescent Psychiatry*, 39, 1468-1484.

LOBLEY, K.J, BEDDELEY, A.D. & GATHERCOLE, S.E. (2005). Phonological similarity effects and verbal complex span. *Psychology Press*, 58 (8), 1462-1478.

LOCKMAN, J.E. & DUNN, S.E. (1993) An intervention and consultation model from a social cognitive perspective: A description of the anger-coping program. *School Psychology Review*, 22, 458-471.

LONG, N. J. (1997). The therapeutic power of kindness. *Reclaiming Children and Youth,* 5 (4), 242-246.

LONGHURST, J., BERKEY, L., & KEYES, B. (2001). Bully-proofing: What one district learned about improving school climate. *Reclaiming Children and Youth*, 9 (4), 224-228.

LOTT, I.T., MCGREGOR, M., ENGELMAN, L., TOUCHETTE, P., TOUMAY, A., SANDMAN, C., FERNANDEZ, G., PLON, L. & WALSH, D. (2004). Longitudinal prescribing patterns for psychoactive medications in community-based individuals with developmental disabilities: Utilization of pharmacy records. *Journal of Intellectual Disability Research*, 48 (6), 563.

LOVELL, C.H. (1992). *Breaking the cycle of poverty.* West Hartford, CT: Kumarian Press.

LYNCH, M.J. (1999). Beating a dead horse: Is there any basic and peer coal evidence for the deterrent effect of imprisonment? *Crime, Law, and Social Change*, 31 (4), 347-362.

MACKENZIE, D. L. & PARENT, D. (1992). Boot camp prisons for young offenders. *Smart sentencing: The emergence of intermediate sanctions.* Newberry Park, CA: Sage Publications.

MACKENZIE, D. L. & HERBERT, E. E. (Eds.) (1996). *Correctional boot camps: A tough intermediate sanction.* Washington, DC: National Institute of Justice.

MACKENZIE, D. L. (1997). Criminal justice and crime prevention. In L. W. Sherman et al. (Eds.) *Preventing crime: What works, what doesn't, what's promising (a Report to the United States Congress).* College Park, MD: Department of Criminology and Criminal Justice, University Of Maryland.

MACKENZIE, D. L., STYVE, G. J., GOVER, A. R., & WILSON, DB (2001). The Impact of boot camps and traditional institutions on juvenile residence: Adjustment, perception of the environment and changes in social bonds, impulsivity, and antisocial attitudes. *Journal on Research in Crime & Delinquency*, 38, 279-313.

MARGOLIN, G. & GORDIS, E.B. (2004). Children's exposure to violence in the family and community. *Current Directions and Psychological Science*, 13 (4), 152.

MASH, E. & JOHNSTON, C. (1983a) Parental perceptions of child behavior problems, parenting self-esteem, and mother's reported stress in younger and older hyperactive and normal children. *Journal of Consulting and Clinical Psychology*, 51, 86-99.

MASH, E.J. & HUNSLEY, J. (2005). Evidence-based assessment of child and adolescent disorders: Issues and challenges. *Journal of Clinical Child & Adolescent Psychology*, 34 (3), 362-379.

MASHAL, N., & KASIRER, A. (2012). Principal component analysis study of visual and verbal metaphoric comprehension in children with autism and learning disabilities. *Research in developmental disabilities*, 33(1), 274-282.

MASLOW, A. (1970). *Motivation and personality.* New York: Harper & Row.

MASLOW, A. H. (1987). *Motivation and personality.* 3rd Edition. New York: Longman.

MASTERS, KJ, BELLONCI, C., et al. (2002). Practice parameters for the prevention and management of aggressive behavior in child and adolescent psychiatric institutions with special reference to seclusion and restraint. *Journal of the American Academy of Child and Adolescent Psychiatry*, 41, 4-25.

MATE, J., LLEN, R. J., & BAQUES, J. (2012). What you say matters: Exploring visual-verbal interactions in visual working memory. *The Quarterly Journal of Experimental Psychology*, 65(3), 395-400.

MATHAN, S. & KOEDINGER, K. (2003). Recasting the feedback debate: Benefits of tutoring error detection and correction skills. Proc. of the International AIED Conference 2003, July 20-24, Sydney, Australia.

MAUGHAN, B., ROWE, R., MESSER, J., GOODMAN, R. & MELTZER, H. (2004). Conduct disorder and oppositional defiant disorder in a national sample: A developmental epidemiology. *Journal of Child Psychology and Psychiatry*, 45, 609.

MAYER, J. D., SALOVEY, P., & CARUSO, D. R. (2008). Emotional intelligence: New ability or eclectic traits?. *American Psychologist, 63*(6), 503.

MAYER, J. D., ROBERTS, R. D., & BARSADE, S. G. (2008). Human abilities: Emotional intelligence. *Annual. Review of Psychology, 59,* 507-536.

MAYES, L.C. (1994). Neurobiology of prenatal cocaine exposure of fact on developing monoamine systems. *Infant Mental Health Journal,* 15 (2), 121-133.

MCDERMOT, B.M. & GIBBON, P. (2002). Embedding categorical constructs in contemporary child mental health approaches. *Australian and New Zealand Journal of Psychiatry,* 36 (4), 481.

MCMAHON, R.J. & SLOUGH, N.M. (1996). Family-based intervention in the FAST track program. In: Peters R.V., MCMAHON, R.J., editors. *Preventing childhood disorders, substance abuse and delinquency.* California: Sage, pp 298-328.

MENDICINO, M., RAZZAQ, L., & HEFFERNAN, N., (2009). A comparison of traditional homework to computer-supported homework. *Journal of Research on Technology in Education, 41*(3), 331-358.

MILNE, J. (2001) Family treatment of oppositional defiant disorder: Changing views and strength-based approaches. *Family Journal,* 9.

MIYAKE, A., FRIEDMAN, N. P., EMERSON, M. J., WITZKI, A. H., HOWETER, A., & WAGER, T. D. (2000). The unity and diversity of executive functions and their contributions to complex "frontal lobe" tasks: A latent variable analysis. *Cognitive Psychology, 41*(1), 49-100.

MORASH, M. & RUCKER, L. (1990). A critical look at the idea of boot camp as a correctional reform. *Crime & Delinquency,* 36, 204-222.

MOUNTS, N. S. (2002). Parental management of adolescent peer relationships in context: The role of parenting style. *Journal of Family Psychology, 16*(1), 58.

MPOFU, E. & CRYSTAL, R. (2001) Conduct disorder in children: Challenges, and prospective cognitive behavioural treatments. *Counseling Psychology Quarterly,* 14.

MULLEN, J. K. (2000). The physical restraint controversy. *Reclaiming Children and Youth,* 9 (2), 92-94, 124.

MURPHY, P. K. & ALEXANDER, P. A. (2000). "A motivated exploration of motivation terminology." *Contemporary Educational Psychology* 25: 3–53.

MURRAY, J.P. (2001) TV violence and brain mapping and children. *Psychiatric Times* 18 (10).

NEWCORN, J.H., SPENCER, TJ, BEIDERMAN, J., MILTON, D. & MICHELSON, D. (2005). Atomoxetine treatment in children and adolescents with attention-deficit/hyperactivity disorder and comorbid oppositional defiant disorder. *Journal of the American Academy of Child & Adolescent Psychiatry,* 44 (3), 240, 248.

NICKEL, M.K., KRAWCZYK, J., NICKEL, C., FORTHUBER, P., KETTLER, C., LEIBERICH, P., MUELBACHER, M., TRITT, K., MITTERLEHNER, F.O., LAHMANN, C., ROTHER, W.K. & LOEW, T.H. (2005). Anger, interpersonal relationships, and health-related quality of life in bullying boys who are treated with outpatient family therapy: A randomized, prospective, controlled trial with 1 year of follow-up. *Pediatrics,* 116 (2), 247-254.

NIJSTAD, B.A., STROEBE, W. & LODEWIJKX, H.F.M. (2003). Production blocking an idea generation: Does blocking interfere with cognitive processes? *Journal of Experimental Social Psychology,* 39 (6), 531-548.

NISBETT, R. & WILSON, T. (1977). Telling more than we can know: Verbal reports on mental processes. *Psychological Review*, 84, 231-259.

OESTERREICH, L. (1995). Ages & stages-five-year-olds. Oesterreich, L., Holt, B. & Karas, S., *Iowa family child care handbook*, 207 -210. Ames, IA: Iowa State University Extension.

OESTERREICH, L. (1995). Ages & stages-six through eight -year-olds. Oesterreich, L., Holt, B. & Karas, S., *Iowa family child care handbook*, 211 -212. Ames, IA: Iowa State University Extension.

OLVERA, R.L. (2002). Intermittent explosive disorder: epidemiology, diagnosis and management. *Central Nervous System Drugs*, 16, 517-526.

ORTIZ, J. & RAINE, A.D. (2004). Heart rate level and antisocial behavior in children and adolescents: A meta-analysis. *Journal of the American Academy of Child & Adolescent Psychiatry*, 43 (2), 154-162.

PS026610, PS026611, PS026612. NATIONAL TELEVISION VIOLENCE STUDY. Volumes 1, 2, and 3. Margaret Seawell, Ed. 1997.

PAPPADOPULOS, E., MACINTYRE, JC, CRISMON, ML, et al. (2003). Treatment recommendations for the use of antipsychotics for aggressive youth. Part II. *Journal of the American Academy of Child and Adolescent Psychiatry*, 42 (2), 145-161

PATTERSON, G.R. & FORGATCH, M.S. (1987) *Parents and adolescents living together*. Oregon: Castalia.

PEREPLETCHIKOVA, F., AXELROD, S. R., KAUFMAN, J., ROUNSAVILLE, B. J., DOUGLAS-PALUMBERI, H., & MILLER, A. L. (2011). Adapting dialectical behaviour therapy for children: Towards a new research agenda for paediatric suicidal and non-suicidal self-injurious behaviours. *Child and adolescent mental health*, 16(2), 116-121.

PETRIDES, K. V., & FURNHAM, A. (2000). On the dimensional structure of emotional intelligence. *Personality and individual differences*, 29(2), 313-320.

PIERCE, J. M., PRIGGS, A. D., GAST, D. L., & LUSCRE, D. (2013). Effects of visual activity schedules on independent classroom transitions for students with autism. *International Journal of Disability, Development and Education*, 60(3), 253-269.

PINTRICH, P.R. (2003). "A motivational science perspective on the role of student motivation." *Journal of Educational Psychology* 95.4: 667–686.

POLLIT, E. & THOMSON, C. (1977). Protein-calorie malnutrition and behavior: A view from psychology. In *Nutrition and the brain*, 2 (Eds.) R.J. Wurthman & J.J. Wurthman. New York: Raven Press.

PRINZ, R. J., BLACHMAN, E. A., & DUMAS, J. E. (1994). An evaluation of peer coping-skills training for childhood aggression. *Journal of clinical child psychology*, 23(2), 193-203.

PROVENCO, E. (1991). *Video game kids: Making sense of Nintendo*. Harvard University Press.

QUIGLEY, R. (2003). The colorful evolution of a strength-based treatment model. *Reclaiming Children and Youth*, 12 (1), 28-32.

RADIGAN, M., LANNON, P., ROOHAN, P. & GESTEN, F. (2005). Medication patterns for attention-deficit/ hyperactivity disorder and comorbid psychiatric conditions in a low-income population. *Journal of Child and Adolescent Psychopharmacology*, 15 (1), 44-56.

RATNER, C. (1993 a). *A socio-historical approach to contextualism*. IN S. HAYES, L. HAYES, H. REESE, & T. SARBIN (Eds.), Varieties of scientific contextualism (169-186). Reno: Context Press.

RAYCHABA, B. (1982). Commentary-"Out of control": A youth perspective unsecured treatments and physical restraint. *Journal of Child and Youth Care*, 7, 83-87.

REGIER, D.A., KAELBER, C.T., RAE, D.S., FARMER, M.E., KNAUPER, B., KESSLER, R.C. & NORQUIST, G.S. (1998). Limitations of diagnostic criteria and assessment instruments for mental disorders: Implications for research and policy. *Archives of General Psychiatry*, 55, 109-115.

ROBERTS, A. C., ROBBINS, T. W., & WEISKRANTZ, L. E. (1998). *The prefrontal cortex: Executive and cognitive functions*. Oxford University Press.

ROBERTS, R. D., SCHULZE, R., O'BRIEN, K., MACCANN, C., REID, J., & MAUL, A. (2006). Exploring the validity of the Mayer-Salovey-Caruso Emotional Intelligence Test (MSCEIT) with established emotions measures. *Emotion*, 6(4), 663.

ROBINS, C. J., & CHAPMAN, A. L. (2004). Dialectical behavior therapy: Current status, recent developments, and future directions. *Journal of personality disorders*, 18(1), 73-89.

RODICK, A. (Ed.) (2003). *A revolution in kindness*. West Sussex, UK: Anita Roddick Books.

ROGERS, S. J., WHENER, E.A. & HAGERMAN, R. (2001). The behavioral phenotype in fragile x: Symptoms of autism in very young children with fragile x syndrome, idiopathic autism, and other developmental disorders. *Journal of Developmental & Behavioral Pediatrics*, 22 (6), 409-417.

ROLLIN, S.A., KAISER-ULREY, C., POTTS, I. & CREASON, A.H. (2003). A school-based violence prevention model for at-risk eighth-grade youth. *Psychology in the Schools*, 40 (4), 403-416.

ROSENBERG, M. (1999). *Nonviolent communication*. Encinitas, CA: Puddle Dancer Press.

ROSS, C. & BLANC, H. (2000) Parenting stress in mothers of young children with Oppositional Defiant Disorder and other severe behavior disorders. *Child Study Journal*, 28.

ROTHEREM-BORUS, M.J. & DUAN, N. (2003). Generation of preventative interventions. *Child and Adolescent Psychiatry*, 42 (5), 518-526.

SAPER, B. (1971). Psycho-economic reinforcement as treatment. *Psychiatric Quarterly*, 45 (3), 458-462.

SAUNDERS, B. J. (2013). Ending the physical punishment of children by parents in the English-speaking world: The impact of language, tradition and law.

SCAHILL, L. & SCHWAB-STONE, M. (2000). Epidemiology of ADHD and school-age children. *Child and Adolescent Psychiatric Clinic North America*, and 9, 541-555.

SCHOLTE, E.M. (1992). Prevention and treatment of juvenile problem behavior: A proposal for a socio-ecological approach. *Journal of Abnormal Child Psychology*, 20 (3), 247-262.

SCHREIBMAN, L., WHALEN, C., & STAHMER, A. C. (2000). The use of video priming to reduce disruptive transition behavior in children with autism. *Journal of Positive Behavior Interventions*, 2(1), 3-11.

SCHUTTE, N. S., MALOUFF, J. M., HALL, L. E., HAGGERTY, D. J., COOPER, J. T., GOLDEN, C. J., & DORNHEIM, L. (1998). Development and validation of a measure of emotional intelligence. *Personality and individual differences*, 25(2), 167-177.

SCHWARTZ, B. (1978). *Psychology of learning and behavior*. New York: W.W. Norton and Company, Inc.

SECHREST, D.D. (1989). Prison "boot camps" do not measure up. *Federal Probation*, 53, 15-20.

SEITA, J. & BRENDTRO, L. (2002). *Kids who outwit adults.* Long Mount, CO: Sopris West.

SELLS, S. P. (1998). *Treating the tough adolescent.* New York: The Guilford Press.

SERKETICH, W.J. & DUMAS, J.E. (1996) The effectiveness of behavioral parent training to modify antisocial behavior in children: A meta-analysis. *Behavior Therapy*, 27, 159-170.

SEIGELMAN, C. & MANSFIELD, K. (1992) Knowledge of and receptivity to psychological treatment in childhood and adolescence. *Journal of Clinical Child Psychology*, 21, 2-9.

SHUTE, V. J. (2007). Focus on formative feedback. Educational Testing Services. Princeton, NJ.

SINGH, R., SALEEM, M., PRADHAN, P., HEFFERNAN, C., HEFFERNAN, N., RAZZAQ, L. DAILY, M., O'CONNER, C. & MULCHAY, C. (2011). Feedback during web-based homework: The role of hints in proceedings of the artificial intelligence in Education Conference 2011. Springer. LNAI 6738, Pages. 328–336.

SOLNICK, J., BRAUKMANN, C., BEDLINGTON, M., KIRIGIN, K. & WOLFE, M. (1981). The relationship between parent-youth interaction and delinquency in group homes. *Journal of Abnormal Child Psychology*, 9 (1), 107-119.

SKINNER, B.F. (1969) *Contingencies of reinforcement: A theoretical analysis.* New York: Meredith Corporation.

SOBEL, D.M., TENENBAUM, J.B. & GOPNIK, A. (2004). Children's causal references from indirect evidence: backwards blocking and Bayesian reasoning in preschoolers. *Cognitive Science: A Multidisciplinary Journal*, 28 (3), 303-333.

STALLER, J.A., WADE, M.J. & BAKER, M. (2005). Current prescribing patterns in outpatient child and adolescent psychiatric practice in Central New York. *Journal of Child and Adolescent Psychopharmacology*, 15 (1), 57-61.

STOCK, G. (1988) *The kid's book of questions.* New York: Workman Publishing.

STORMSHACK, E. (2000) Parenting practices and child disruptive behavior problems in early elementary school. *Journal of Clinical Psychology*, 29.

STUSS, D. T., & KNIGHT, R. T. (Eds.). (2013). *Principles of frontal lobe function.* Oxford University Press.

STYVE, G.J., MACKENZIE, D.L., GOVER, A.R. & MITCHELL, O. (2000). Perceived conditions of confinement: A national of valuation of juvenile boot camps and traditional facilities. *Law and Human Behavior*, 24 (3), 297-308.

THOMPSON, C.L. & RUDOLPH, L..B (1996) *Counseling children* (Fourth Edition). Pacific Grove, CA: Brooks/Cole Publishing.

THOMPSON, T. & GRABOWSKI, J.G. (1972) *Reinforcement schedules and multi-operant analysis.* New York: Meredith Corporation.

TREMBLAY, R.E., VITARO, F., BERTRAND, L., LEBLANC, M., BEAUCHESNE, H. & BIOLEAU, H. (1992) Parent and child training to prevent early onset of delinquency: the Montreal longitudinal study. In: MCCORD, J. & TREMBLAY, R.E. (Eds.) *Parenting antisocial behavior: Interventions from birth through adolescence.* New York: Guilford.

TRIESCHMAN, A.E., WHITAKER, J.K. & BRENDTRO, L.K. (1969). *The other 23 hours.* New York: Aldine de Gruyter.

TSAL, Y., SHALEV, L. & MEVORACH, C. (2005). The diversity of attention deficits in ADHD: The prevalence of four cognitive factors and ADHD versus controls. *Journal of Learning Disability*, 38 (2), 142-157.

TURKLE, S. (1984). *The second self: Computers and the human spirit.* London: Granada.

VANDERVEN, K. (2000). Cultural aspects of point and level systems. *Reclaiming children and youth*, 9 (1), 53-59.

VAN DE WIEL, N., VAN GOOZEN, S., MATTHYS, W., SNOEK, H., & VAN ENGELAND, H. (2004). Cortisol and treatment effect in children with disruptive behavior disorders: A preliminary study. *Journal of the American Academy of Child & Adolescent Psychiatry*, 43 (8), 1011-1018.

VAN DER KOLK, BA, DUCEY, CP. (1989) The psychological processing of traumatic experience: Rorschach patterns in PTSD. *Journal of Traumatic Stress,* 2: 259-274.

VAN DER KOLK, BA, PERRY, JC, HERMAN, JL. (1991) Childhood origins of self- destructive behavior. *American Journal of Psychiatry,* 148:1665-1671.

VAN DER KOLK, BA & VAN DER HART, O. (1991) *The intrusive past: The flexibility of memory and the engraving of trauma.* American Imago: 48:425-454.

VORRATH, H.H. & BRENDTRO, LK (1974). *Positive peer culture.* New York: Aldine de Gruyter. Second edition published 1985.

WAGNER, A. D., MARIL, A., BJORK, R. A., & SCHACTER, D. L. (2001). Prefrontal contributions to executive control: fMRI evidence for functional distinctions within lateral prefrontal cortex. *Neuroimage, 14*(6), 1337-1347.

WEAKLAND, J., FISH, R., WATZLAWICK, P. & BODIN, A. (1974). Brief therapy: Focused problem resolution. *Family Process*, 13, 141-168.

WEAKLAND, J. (1976) *Communication therapy and clinical change.* In: GUERIN, P. (Ed.) Family Therapy (pp 111-128). New York: Gardener.

WEBB, C. A., SCHWAB, Z. J., WEBER, M., DELDONNO, S., KIPMAN, M., WEINER, M. R., & KILGORE, W. D. (2013). Convergent and divergent validity of integrative versus mixed model measures of emotional intelligence. *Intelligence, 41*(3), 149-156.

WEEMS, C.F., SALTZMAN, K.M., REISS, A.L. & CARRION, V.G. (2003). A prospective test of the association between hyper or arousal and emotional numbing in youth with a history of traumatic stress. *Journal of Clinical Child and Adolescent Psychology*, 32 (1), 166-171.

WEISSENBERGER, A.A., DELL, M. L., LIOW, K., THEODORE, W., FRATTALI, C.M., HERNANDEZ, D. & ZAMETKIN, A. (2001). Aggression and psychiatric comorbidity and children with hypothalamus hamartomas and their unaffected siblings. *Journal of the American Academy of Child & Adolescent Psychiatry*, 40 (6), 696-703.

WERTSCH, J. (1985 a). *Culture, communication, and cognition: Vygotskian perspectives.* New York: Cambridge University Press.

WIEST, D.J., et al. (2001). "Intrinsic motivation among regular, special, and alternative education high school students." *Adolescence*: 111–126.

WIGFIELD, A. & ECCLES, J.S. (2000). "Expectancy-value theory of achievement motivation." *Contemporary Educational Psychology*: 68–81.

WILENS, T.E., SPENCER, T. J., BEIDERMAN, J & SCHLEIFER, D. (1997). Case study: Nefazodone for juvenile mood disorders. *Journal of the American Academy of Child & Adolescent Psychiatry*, 36 (4), 481-485.

WILLS, T.A., BLECHMAN, E.A., & MCNEMARA, G. (1996). Family support, coping, and competence.

WILKE-DEATON, J.L. (2006) *Creative parenting skills: The training handbook.* PESI Healthcare: Eau Claire, WI.

WILSON, J. (2005). Boot camps and effectiveness. *American Journal of Psychiatry*, 161, 184.

WOLIN, S. (2003). What is a strength? *Reclaiming Children and Youth*, 12 (1), 18-21.

WOOLLEY, G. (2007). A comprehension intervention for children with reading comprehension difficulties. *Australian Journal of Learning Difficulties*, *12*(1), 43-50.

WOOLLEY, G. (2010). Developing reading comprehension: Combining visual and verbal cognitive processes. *Australian Journal of Language and Literacy, The*, *33*(2), 108.

RIGHT, S. (1999). Physical restraint in the management of violence and aggression in in-patient settings: a review of issues. *Journal of Mental Health*, 8 (5), 459-472.

YALOM, I.D. (2002) *The gift of therapy*, New York: HarperCollins Publishers.

YALOM, I.D. & YALOM, B. (Ed.) (1998) *The Yalom reader: Selections from the work of a master therapist and storyteller.* New York: Perseus Books.

YALOM, I.D. (1995) *The theory and practice of group psychotherapy* (Fourth Edition). New York: Basic Books.

YATES, A.J. (1975) *Theory and practice in behavior therapy.* Canada: John Wiley & Sons, Inc.

ZAHN, T.P. & KRUESI, M.J. (1993). Autonomic activity and boys with disruptive behavior disorders. *Psychophysiology*, 33 (4), 612-628.

ZILLMAN, D. (1993). Mental control of angry aggression. In D.M. WEGNER & J.W. PENEBAKER (Eds.), *Handbook of mental control* (370-392). Upper Saddle River, New Jersey: Prentice-Hall.